1/13/09

CHECK YOUR ENGLISH VOCABULARY FOR

TOEFL®

by

Rawdon Wyatt

THIRD EDITION

A & C Black • London

www.acblack.com

First edition published in Great Britain 2002
Second edition published in 2004
This third edition published in 2007

A & C Black Publishers Ltd
38 Soho Square, London W1D 3HB

© Rawdon Wyatt 2007

A CIP entry for this book is available from the British Library.
ISBN-10: 0 7136 8414 3
ISBN-13: 978 0 7136 8414 8

Text typeset by A & C Black
Printed in Great Britain by Martins the Printers, Berwick upon Tweed

This book is produced using paper that is made from wood grown in managed, sustainable forests. It is natural, renewable and recyclable. The logging and manufacturing processes conform to the environmental regulations of the country of origin.

Introduction

If you are going to take the TOEFL®, you will find the vocabulary exercises in this workbook very helpful. They will help you to review, practice and acquire a lot of the words and expressions that you might need to use in the Writing and Speaking sections, or that you might come across or be tested on in the Listening and Reading sections. A greater command of vocabulary is one of the key factors that will help you raise your TOEFL® score.

Structure of the workbook

The workbook is divided into 2 sections. The first section deals with general vocabulary, including synonyms, idioms and phrasal verbs. The second, smaller section is topic-specific, and focuses on some of the topics that regularly appear in the TOEFL®. Each topic is accompanied by a typical TOEFL® Writing question, which will give you the chance to use the key vocabulary in an essay.
There is a comprehensive answer key at the back of the book.

How to use the book

You should not go through the exercises mechanically. It is better to choose areas that you are unfamiliar with, or areas that you feel are of specific interest or importance to yourself. Remember that you should keep a record of new words and expressions that you learn, and review these from time to time so that they become an active part of your vocabulary. There is a vocabulary record sheet at the back of the book which you can photocopy as many times as you like. Use this to build up your own personal vocabulary bank.
It is essential to have a good dictionary with you when you are doing the exercises. For basic vocabulary, we recommend the **American English Study Dictionary** (ISBN 978 1 9016 5969 6). For a more advanced and in-depth coverage of vocabulary, the **Macmillan English Dictionary** (ISBN 978 1 4050 2628 4), from which many of the sample sentences in this book are taken, is ideal.

Extending your vocabulary

Also remember that there are other methods of acquiring new vocabulary. For example, you should read as much as possible from a different variety of authentic reading materials (books, newspapers, magazines, etc).

Practicing for the TOEFL

There is a lot of TOEFL material available, but we particularly recommend **Barron's TOEFL iBT** (ISBN 978 0 7641 3374 9), which provides comprehensive practice for all sections of the exam, as well as offering essential language skills development and useful studying strategies. It also gives lots of vital information on the test itself and how it works. The book has been written for the Internet-based TOEFL, but is also useful if you are going to take the older, standard computer-based TOEFL.

Information about the TOEFL®

The purpose of the TOEFL® is to evaluate a non-native English speaker's proficiency in the English language. Almost one million students every year from 180 countries register to take the TOEFL®: the majority of universities and colleges in North America as well as in other English-speaking countries require official TOEFL® score reports for admission. The test is also used by institutions in other countries where English is the language of instruction. In addition, government agencies, scholarship programs and licensing / certification agencies use TOEFL® scores to evaluate English proficiency. An acceptable score depends on the particular institution or agency involved.

About the Check your English Vocabulary series

Check your English Vocabulary for TOEFL® is one of several books in the *Check your English Vocabulary* series. These books are designed to help students of English (and those who are working or who want to work in an English-speaking environment) to develop and practice the essential vocabulary that they would need to know or use on a day-to-day basis, or in order to get a better grade in an exam.

There are currently 16 books in the series:

Check your Vocabulary for Academic English
Check your English Vocabulary for TOEFL®
Check your English Vocabulary for TOEIC
Check your English Vocabulary for IELTS
Check your English Vocabulary for FCE+
Check your Vocabulary for English for the PET Examination
Check your English Vocabulary for Phrasal Verbs and Idioms
Check your English Vocabulary for Business and Administration
Check your English Vocabulary for Law
Check your English Vocabulary for Medicine
Check your English Vocabulary for Computers and Information Technology
Check your English Vocabulary for Leisure, Travel and Tourism
Check your English Vocabulary for Human Resources
Check your English Vocabulary for Banking and Finance
Check your English Vocabulary for Living in the UK
Check your Vocabulary for Natural English Collocations

For more information, visit **www.acblack.com**

Contents

Addition, equation, and conclusion

This exercise will help you to review more of the important words that we use to join ideas in an essay, a verbal presentation or sometimes in everyday speech.

Exercise 1
Put the following words and expressions into their correct place in the table depending on their function.

| to sum up briefly • along with • as well as • it can be concluded that |
| likewise • similarly • also • too • in addition • besides • to conclude |
| in brief • in the same way • thus • what's more • furthermore |
| moreover • along with • to summarize • therefore • correspondingly |

Addition (For example: *and*)	Equation (For example: *equally*)	Conclusion (For example: *in conclusion*)

Exercise 2
Complete these sentences with one of the words or expressions from above. In most cases, more than one answer is possible.

1.   Tourism brings much needed money to developing countries. _____, it provides employment for the local population.

2.   _____ bringing much needed money to developing countries, tourism provides employment for the local population.

3.   Tourists should respect the local environment. _____ they should respect the local customs.

4.   _____ industrial waste, pollution from car fumes is poisoning the environment.

5.   In order to travel, you need a passport. _____, you might need a visa, immunization shots, and written permission to visit certain areas.

6.   Drugs are banned in Britain. _____ weapons such as guns and knives.

7.   All power corrupts. _____, absolute power corrupts absolutely.

8.   You shouldn't smoke, drink, take drugs, or eat unhealthy food. _____, you should live a more healthy lifestyle.

9.   The ozone layer is becoming depleted, the air in the cities is becoming too dirty to breathe, and our seas and rivers are no longer safe to swim in. _____ pollution is slowly destroying the planet.

10. Your grades have been very poor all year. _____ you need to work really hard if you want to pass your exams next month.

American English

This exercise looks at some common "American" words (words which are used in the U.S.A. and Canada). You might find it useful if you have been learning "British" English (the English which is spoken in the United Kingdom and in other countries around the world). Generally, "American" words are understood by "British" English speakers (largely as a result of imported television programs and movies), but many North Americans are unfamiliar with some "British" English words. As a result, it is important to use the "American" words rather than the "British" words in the TOEFL.

Look at the sentences below, which all contain a "British" English word in **bold**. Decide what word North Americans would normally use in the same context. In some cases, the word will remain the same, but there will be a difference in spelling. Write your answers in the crossword grid on page 7. To help you, the word that you need has been put at the end of each sentence, with most of the letters removed, but with some of the letters included.

<u>Across</u> (⇨)

2.   The play is in two acts, with a short **interval** between the two.   I _ T _ _ M _ _ _ _ _ N

6.   If you make a mistake in your calculations, you'll need to do them **again**.   _ V _ _

8.   The **post** normally arrives before lunchtime.   _ _ _ L

9.   The government refused to **recognise** the new republic.   _ E _ _ _ _ _ _ _

11.   The **theatre** received an unexpected grant which helped to prevent it closing down.   _ H _ _ _ _ _

13.   The road outside the school is very busy, so students are advised to use the **subway** to cross it.
        _ N _ _ _ P _ _ _

16.   The oil crisis resulted in a 28% rise in the cost of **petrol**.   _ _ S

18.   Take the **lift** to the top floor.   _ _ _ V _ _ O _

20.   **Estate agents** are some of the most unscrupulous people in the country.   R _ _ L _ _ R _

24.   The M40 is closed, so you will need to take the A40, which is the **main road** connecting London with Oxford.   H _ _ _ W _ _

26.   Their request for a $2 **rise** in the hourly rate was firmly rejected by the management.   _ A _ _ E

27.   The workshop will last for 6 hours, with a **break** for lunch at midday.   _ E _ _ S _

29.   (*Informal*) I really like Mr. Goldberg. He's a great **bloke**.   _ U _

30.   (*At a school, college, or university*) A **staff** meeting has been called for two o'clock.   _ _ C _ _ _ Y

32.   In my opinion, the best time of the year is **autumn**.   _ _ L _

35.   The automobile company's first attempt to design a family **saloon** that ran on diesel was a resounding failure.   _ _ D _ N

36.   The campus has a **shop** where students can buy stationery and essential items.   _ _ O _ _

37.   Government spending on **defence** was reduced by 23%.   _ _ _ E _ _ _

38. He gave me just enough money to buy a **return** bus ticket to Portland.   R _ _ _ D - _ _ _ P
    (*2 words, which are hyphenated. Do not leave a gap or use a hyphen in the crossword grid*)

40. He's a **graduate** of Berkeley College.   _ _ _ M N _ _

41. These days it is not unusual to see children as young as five carrying a **mobile phone** to school.
    C _ _ _ _ _ _ N _

Down (⬌)

1. The **postcode** for the company is MA 04532.   _ I _   _ O _ _
   (*2 words: do not leave a gap between the words in the crossword grid*)

3. Classes start at nine o'clock every morning Monday **to** Friday.   T _ R _ _ _ _

4. There are several museums and galleries in the city, but most students prefer to spend their evenings
   at the **cinema**.   _ _ V _ E _

5. Have you got any change for a $20 **note**?   B _ _ _

7. Strict **labour** laws have had an adverse effect on small businesses.   _ _ B _ _

10. I'm afraid we've **got** slightly behind schedule.   _ _ T T _ _

12. Several **flats** were leased to private agencies, who in turn leased them to small companies.
    _ P _ _ T _ _ _ _ _

14. All **travellers** flying to the USA have to undergo strict security checks at the airport.
    _ _ A _ _ _ _ _ _

15. The Dean's office is on the **ground** floor.   _ I _ _ _

17. The first thing the council did was dig up the **pavement** outside the front door.   _ _ D _ W _ _ _

19. My favorite **film** of all time has to be the classic 1959 comedy 'Some Like It Hot'.   _ _ V _ _

21. The best way to get from one part of the city to another is to use the **dual carriageway**.
    _ _ E _ W _ _

22. (*On the telephone, when you are calling someone*) Hello, is **that** Harrison Keane?   _ _ _ S

23. In the event of a marital divorce or separation, there is a clear need for **dialogue** between the
    parents and their children.   _ _ A _ _ _

25. If you want to stop smoking, the best place to start is by going to your local **chemist**.
    D _ _ G _ _ _ _ _

28. Services on the **underground** start at five in the morning and finish at half past midnight.
    _ _ B _ _ Y

31. Before buying a house, it is essential to employ the services of a good **solicitor**.   _ T T _ _ _ _ _

33. You should use a pencil to do the test, and use a **rubber** to remove any mistakes.   _ _ A _ _ _

34. Most Americans tend to stay in the country for their **holiday**.   V _ _ _ T _ _ _

39. You don't need to ask me for permission to use the **toilet**!   B _ _ _ R _ _ _

Changes

<u>Exercise 1</u>

Look at these sentences and decide if the statement which follows each one is <u>true</u> or <u>false</u>. Use the words and expressions in **bold** to help you decide.

1. The population of the country has trebled in the last 25 years.
   *There has been a **dramatic increase** in the number of people living in the country.*

2. Unemployment has dropped by about 2% every year for the last six years.
   *There has been a **steady decrease** in the number of people out of work.*

3. The government has spent a lot of money improving roads around the country.
   *There has been a **deterioration** in the national road system.*

4. The number of exam passes achieved by the school's pupils has risen by almost 50%.
   *There has been a **decline** in the number of exam passes.*

5. American travelers abroad have discovered that they can buy more foreign currency with their dollar.
   *There has been a **weakening** of the dollar.*

6. It is now much easier to import goods into the country than it was a few years ago.
   *There has been a **tightening up** of border controls.*

7. We're increasing our stocks of coal before the winter begins.
   *We're **running down** our stocks of coal.*

8. Prices have gone up by about 4% every year since 1998.
   *There has been a **constant rise** in the rate of inflation.*

9. The pass rate for the exam was 3% lower this year than it was last year.
   *There has been a **sharp fall** in the pass rate.*

10. The alliance are going to reduce the number of conventional weapons in their armed forces.
    *The alliance are going to **build up** the number of weapons they have.*

11. Deflation has adversely affected industries around the country.
    *There has been a **growth** in industrial activity.*

12. The rules are much stricter now than they were before.
    *There has been a **relaxation** of the rules.*

13. Last year, 12% of the population worked in industry and 10% worked in agriculture. This year, 14% of the population work in industry and 8% work in agriculture.
    *There has been a **narrowing of the gap** between those working in different sectors of the economy.*

14. Some management roles in the company will not exist this time next year.
    *Some management roles are going to be **phased out**.*

15. More people are shopping at large supermarkets rather than small local stores.
    *There has been an **upward trend** in the number of people shopping in small local stores.*

16. Her English is clearly better now than it was when she first arrived.
    *There has been **marked progress** in her English.*

17. People live in better houses, drive nicer cars, and eat higher-quality food than they did twenty years ago.
    *There has been a **general improvement** in the standard of living.*

18. Our company has opened new factories in Detroit, Houston, and Des Moines in the last five years.
    *Our company has witnessed considerable **expansion** in the last five years.*

19. The government will spend less on the healthcare services next year.
    *There are going to be **cuts** in healthcare spending next year.*

20. Americans nowadays want to see more of the world.
    *Americans nowadays want to **narrow** their horizons.*

Exercise 2

The box below contains 31 more words used to describe change in different situations. These are all verbs, and they can be found by reading from left to right and from right to left, starting in the top-left corner and following the direction of the arrows. Separate these words, then use some of them to complete sentences 1 – 10 below. In some cases you will need to change the form of the verb (for example, by putting it into its past simple or past participle form).

⇨	a	d	a	p	t	r	e	p	l	a	c	e	e	x	p	a	n	d	p	r	⇲
⬉	m	r	o	f	s	n	a	r	t	e	c	u	d	e	r	e	t	o	m	o	⬋
⬐	s	w	i	t	c	h	r	e	n	o	v	a	t	e	e	x	c	h	a	n	⇲
⬉	e	p	p	a	s	i	d	r	e	t	l	a	e	t	o	m	e	d	e	g	⬋
⬐	a	r	v	a	r	y	r	a	i	s	e	l	o	w	e	r	e	x	t	e	⇲
⬉	n	e	l	n	e	t	h	g	i	e	h	e	g	r	a	l	n	e	d	n	⬋
⬐	g	t	h	e	n	d	e	e	p	e	n	s	h	o	r	t	e	n	s	t	⇲
⬉	o	t	u	c	d	n	e	m	a	e	s	i	v	e	r	h	c	t	e	r	⬋
⬐	u	t	s	o	u	r	c	e	d	e	t	e	r	i	o	r	a	t	e	s	⇲
⬉	t	s	e	r	e	d	a	r	g	p	u	e	n	i	l	m	a	e	r	t	⬋
⬐	r	u	c	t	u	r	e	d	o	w	n	s	i	z	e	**END**					

1. The company cannot refund customers' money, and goods can only be _____ on production of a receipt or other proof of purchase.

2. We have made radical changes to college regulations, and students are expected to _____ to these over the next few weeks.

3. The discovery of oil _____ the country from a small emirate to a major economic power.

4. The science building is currently being _____, but will remain open while building work is carried out.

5. After only three weeks on the History course, she decided to _____ to something more practical.

6. Fees _____ according to the length of the course: the longer the course, the more you pay.

7. As water freezes, it _____.

8. The economic situation is _____ rapidly, and the entire economy is in danger of collapse.

9. Course fees will be _____ on January 14: some will come down, but most of them will go up.

10. Elastic becomes weaker the more it is _____.

Comparing and Contrasting

Complete these sentences with the most appropriate word or expression in **bold**. In one case, all three options are possible.

1. The **contrast / compare / comparison** in working conditions between our Denver department and our department in Chicago is very noticeable, and employees are now demanding equality in this area.

2. The two engines **differentiate / differ / different** considerably from each other: one runs on gasoline, and the other is a gasoline-electric hybrid.

3. It is often difficult to **differentiate / differ / contrast** between students who are absent because they are genuinely sick, and those who are just enjoying a day in bed.

4. The new software program shared some common **characters / characterizes / characteristics** with those that were already on the market.

5. There's a clear **distinguish / distinctive / distinction** between studying at a college and working from home on a correspondence course.

6. **Compared / Compare / Comparing** with 15 years ago, home PCs are cheaper, faster, and have a much bigger memory.

7. The two courses are different in every way: there's absolutely no **compare / comparison / contrast** between them.

8. Our digital photography course is **similar to / alike / resemble** our traditional photography course, except that it is obviously more computer-oriented.

9. There were several **similarities / similarly / similar to** between the two novels, except one was aimed at a younger market while the other targeted twenty-somethings.

10. Serious computer hackers can access your personal files and destroy or alter them. **Exactly / In the same way / Just as**, they can gain access to your Internet banking facility and steal your money.

11. The quality of his work is excellent. **Likewise / Alike / Likeness**, his attitude and commitment.

12. The TOEFL covers a variety of academic and general English tasks. **In contrast to / Although / By way of contrast**, the TOEIC focuses more on business and professional issues.

13. Grades have not been good over the last semester. **Nevertheless / Even so / However**, the college still has one of the best academic records in the state.

14. There currently seems to be a large **discrepancy / discrimination / differential** between the number of people employed in service industries, and those employed in the primary sector.

15. The Impressionists used light and color to give the general feeling of a scene, **unlike / whereas / whereby** the pre-Raphaelites used a lot of detail and bright colors, and showed a romanticized view of life.

Condition and requirement

Rearrange the letters in **bold** to make words and expressions related to condition and requirement. The first one has been done as an example.

1. **sa nlgo sa** there is sufficient demand for healthy food such as salads and soups in the school cafeteria, we will continue to provide it.
    (**Answer = As long as**)

2. **seusln** I receive your assignment within the next couple of days, I will have to give you a lower grade for the course.

3. Students may use the college computers for personal emails **no incotnido atth** they agree to give up their computer if someone needs it for coursework.

4. Everyone should get a good mid-term grade **vogrnipid ttha** they hand in all their work on time.

5. The main **retncopiinsod** for a healthy economy are controlled consumer spending and low unemployment.

6. (*Notice on a fire alarm*): **ni eacs fo** fire, break glass.

7. **ni het nvete fo** a tie between the two teams in tonight's game, there will be a replay on Saturday afternoon.

8. We agreed to sign the contract, the only **aputonstili** being that it would run for at least five years.

9. The teachers have **nidncoalitoun** trust in their students: they know they will do their best at all times, even if things get difficult.

10. **sumsagin hatt** the flight is on time, we will meet you at LaGuardia airport at ten o'clock.

11. His argument was based **no teh autonmsspi hatt** people are basically decent and honest.

12. Good language skills are one of the **quereesisitpr** for a job in an international organization.

13. Before you accept a job, it is important that you agree with the **remst** and **ioctnsodin** set out in the contract.

14. It is a **nmreiretque** of the college that students attend at least 95% of their course and complete all their assignments on time.

15. If you have a query, please telephone us at the number above. **niifagl ttha**, send us a fax or email.

16. We need to involve at least 20 people on this project, **ehewotris** it can't go ahead.

11

Confusing words and false friends

<u>Confusing words</u> are two or more words which have a similar meaning to each other but are used in a different way.

or

are related to the same topic, but have a different meaning

or

look similar, but have a different meaning

<u>False friends</u> are words in English which have a similar-looking word in another language but which have a different meaning.

Complete the following sentences with the appropriate word in **bold**.

1.   **action / activity**
     The police took immediate _____ when they realised the situation was getting out of hand.
     Economic _____ stagnated as the recession took hold.

2.   **advice / advise**
     Can you _____ me on the best course of action to take?
     He offered me some excellent _____ .

3.   **affect / effect**
     Cuts in spending will have a serious _____ on the healthcare services.
     The strike will seriously _____ train services.

4.   **appreciable / appreciative**
     There is an _____ difference between manslaughter and murder.
     She was very _____ of our efforts to help.

5.   **assumption / presumption**
     They raised taxes on the _____ that it would help control spending.
     It's sheer _____ for the government to suggest things have improved since they came to power.

6.   **avoid / prevent**
     Rapid government reforms managed to _____ a revolution taking place.
     He's always trying to _____ taking a decision if he can help it.

7.   **beside / besides**
     The office is just _____ the railway station.
     _____ their regular daytime job, many people do extra work in the evening.

8.   **briefly / shortly**
     _____ before the conflict began, the army pulled down the border posts.
     The senator spoke _____ about the need for political reform.

9.   **channel / canal**
     The television _____ received a formal complaint about the program.
     The Suez _____ was built in the second half of the nineteenth century.

10. **conscientious / conscious**
     Most people are _____ of the need to protect the environment.
     _____ workers should be rewarded for their hard work.

11. **continual / continuous**
     A _____ trade embargo has badly affected the economic infrastructure.
     The computer has given us _____ problems ever since we installed it.

12. **control / inspect**
Environmental health officers regularly _____ kitchens and other food preparation areas.
The government plans to _____ the price of meat to make sure it doesn't go up too much.

13. **criticism(s) / objection(s)**
They didn't raise any _____ when we insisted on inspecting the figures.
The government's plan was met with severe _____.

14. **damage / injury / harm**
It was a severe _____ which needed immediate hospital treatment.
A lot of _____ was caused to buildings along the coast during the storm.
There's no _____ in taking a break from your job now and then.

15. **discover / invent**
When did he _____ the telephone?
Did Alexander Fleming _____ penicillin?

16. **during / for / while**
Stores were closed _____ the duration of the conflict.
_____ the transition from a dictatorship to democracy, the country experienced severe strikes and riots.
The bomb went off _____ the President was making his speech.

17. **however / moreover**
The plan was good in theory. _____, in practice it was extremely difficult to implement.
The plan was excellent. _____, it was clear from the beginning that it was going to be a success.

18. **considerate / considerable**
He made a _____ amount of money from his dotcom enterprise.
She's a very _____ person, so she would never intentionally upset anyone.

19. **intolerable / intolerant**
I consider his behavior to be quite _____.
The government is _____ of other political parties.

20. **job / work**
Everybody has the right to a decent _____ with good pay.
Following the recession, many people are still looking for _____.

21. **lay(s) / lie(s)**
The city of Quito _____ near the equator.
The manager made it clear he intended to _____ down some strict rules.

22. **look at / watch**
We must _____ the situation in Lugumba carefully, and be prepared to act if violence flares again.
We need to _____ the problem carefully and decide if there is anything we can do about it.

23. **permission / permit**
I'm afraid we can't _____ photography in here.
They received _____ to attend the sessions as long as they didn't interrupt.

24. **possibility / chance**
There is always the _____ that the government will reverse its decision.
If we act now, we have a good _____ of finding a cure for the disease.

25. **priceless / worthless**

_____ paintings by artists like Van Gogh should not be in the hands of private collectors.

As inflation spiraled out of control, paper money suddenly became _____.

26. **principal(s) / principle(s)**

Many people refuse to eat meat on _____.

The _____ of the college is an ardent non-smoker.

The country's _____ products are paper and wood.

Not many people are familiar with the _____ of nuclear physics.

27. **process / procession**

The _____ made its way down the avenue.

Applying for a visa can be a long and frustrating _____.

28. **raise / rise**

As prices _____, demand usually drops.

In response to the current oil shortage, most airlines plan to _____ their fares.

29. **respectable / respectful**

The delegates listened in _____ silence as the chairman spoke.

They want to bring up their children in an area which is considered to be _____.

30. **treat / cure**

Hospitals are so understaffed that they find it almost impossible to _____ patients with minor injuries.

They were unable to _____ the disease, and hundreds died as a result.

31. **subjective / objective**

Your report should be as _____ possible: just present the facts and try to avoid saying what you think about them.

The newspaper article was extremely _____: the journalist more or less forced his own views and ideas on his readership.

32. **disinterested / uninterested**

In order to end the dispute, we need some impartial advice from a / an _____ third party.

I thought they would enjoy my talk, but they were completely _____.

33. **imply / infer**

From what you just said, can I _____ that you think I'm interfering?

I didn't mean to _____ that you were interfering. I merely said that I needed a bit of time to myself.

34. **complimentary / complementary**

In western societies, acupuncture and hypnosis are seen as _____ medicines.

All new students will receive a _____ study pack and dictionary.

Idioms and colloquialisms 1

Idioms and colloquialisms (spoken expressions) are a common feature of the TOEFL Listening Comprehension. There are a lot of them, and each one has to be learnt individually. Often, but not always, it is possible to identify the meaning of an idiom or a colloquialism from the context in which it is being used.

The idioms and colloquialisms exercises in this book focus on some of the most commonly-used expressions.

<u>Exercise 1</u>
Complete the dialogs with an expression from the box.

> I couldn't agree more. • I couldn't care less. • I really don't mind. It's up to you.
> It does nothing for me. • Let me sleep on it. • Never mind. It can't be helped.
> No way! Not a chance! • You've got to be kidding! • Why not? Go for it!
> Wow! Way to go! • You should really get a life. • You're welcome, but it was nothing really.

1. A. Shall we eat out or do you want me to cook something?
    B. _____
    A. OK. In that case, let's eat out.

2. A. The economics seminar has been canceled yet again.
    B. _____
    A. I'm afraid not. Professor Parkhill sure seems to be absent a lot these days.

3. A. Our history lessons are really boring, aren't they.
    B. _____
    A. Right. Perhaps we shouldn't have chosen it as an option.

4. A. We're going to Mo's bar tonight. Want to come?
    B. _____
    A. Come on, don't be like that! It'll be fun!

5. A. I need a decision as soon as possible.
    B. _____
    A. Well, to be honest, I'd rather you told me now.

6. A. Are you interested in science?
    B. _____
    A. Me neither. I find it really boring.

7. A. I spent most of the weekend lying in bed and watching TV.
    B. _____
    A. I know! You're not the first person to say that.

8. A. If you don't work harder, you'll fail your exams.
    B. _____
    A. Well, you should. Your whole future might depend on them.

9. A. I've passed all my exams – grade A's all round!
    B. _____
    A. Thanks. I never thought I'd be able to do it.

10. A. Do you think I should apply to the University of West Virginia?
    B. _____
    A. All right, I will. Thanks.

11. A. Thank you so much for all your help. I couldn't have done it without you.
    B. _____
    A. No, really, I really appreciate it.

12. A. I'm really sorry that I lost your dictionary.
    B. _____
    A. Nevertheless, I promise to replace it.

<u>Exercise 2</u>
Instructions as above.

Let me lend a hand. • How's it going? • How should I know?
I'm a bit tied up for the time being. • I'm going to give it all I've got. • Is it any wonder?
Oh, I'm used to it. • Sure. Why not? • What a drag! • What do you have in mind?
You bet! • You're out of luck.

---

1.   A. Can I have a look at your essay to get a few ideas?
     B. _____
     A. Thanks. I'll do the same for you next time.

2.   A. I'm working really hard for my exam at the moment.
     B. _____
     A. Oh, not bad. I'm fairly confident of passing.

3.   A. Where's Murai today?
     B. _____
     A. Don't be like that. I was only asking.

4.   A. We need to finish this assignment by Monday. There goes our weekend.
     B. _____
     A. I know, but we'll make up for it next weekend.

5.   A. Want to come to the concert tonight?
     B. _____
     A. That's great. I'll go and get us some tickets.

6.   A. Do you think you'll pass your exams?
     B. _____
     A. That's the spirit! Well, good luck.

7.   A. Do you find it difficult getting up at 6 o'clock every morning?
     B. _____
     A. I suppose you must be. You've been doing it for so long.

8.   A. We're thinking of doing something to celebrate the end of the semester.
     B. _____
     A. I'm not sure, really. Perhaps a barbecue, or something like that.

9.   A. Are there any tickets left for tonight's show?
     B. _____
     A. I thought so. Oh well, never mind.

10.   A. I have to get the hall ready for tonight's lecture.
     B. _____
     A. That's really kind of you.

11.   A. I was wondering if you could help me with my assignment.
     B. _____
     A. Yes, I thought you might be a bit busy right now.

12.   A. Poor Sarah failed to get a good grade in her TOEFL once again.
     B. _____
     A. Right. She never seems to do any preparation for it.

Idioms and colloquialisms 2

Exercise 1
Complete these dialogs with an appropriate expression from the box.

> A little bird told me. • Be my guest. • Fire away, I'm all ears. • I'd be glad to
> I'm having second thoughts. • I'm keeping my fingers crossed. • My lips are sealed.
> Now you're talking! • Rather you than me. • That'll be the day! • That'll teach you!
> Who let the cat out of the bag?

1. A. Would you mind looking after my bag while I go to the rest room?
    B. _____

2. A. Do you mind if I sit here?
    B. _____

3. A. How do you know the test has been canceled?
    B. _____

4. A. I'd be really grateful if you didn't tell anyone about it.
    B. _____

5. A. Do you think you'll pass the exam?
    B. _____

6. A. I've signed up for extra sociology classes with Professor Dullman.
    B. _____

7. A. I've got some really interesting news.
    B. _____

8. A. You don't want to work tonight? OK, let's go to the theater instead.
    B. _____

9. A. I thought you were going to apply for a place on the Theory of Knowledge course.
    B. _____

10. A. I promise to work harder from now on.
    B. _____

11. A. I hear that you're going to throw a surprise party for my birthday.
    B. _____

12. A. I've just eaten six hot dogs, and now I've got a terrible stomach ache.
    B. _____

Exercise 2
Instructions as above.

> Congratulations. • Couldn't be better. • Hold on. • I'd love to. • I'd rather you didn't.
> Oh, that's too bad. • Oh, this is on me. • Sure, touch wood.
> Thanks. Make yourself at home. • The name doesn't ring any bells. • You're welcome.
> Yes. Take care and keep in touch.

1. A. I can't afford to go to the concert tonight.
    B. _____

2. A. I've managed to get a place on the Advanced Studies program.
    B. _____

3. A. Would you like to come to Gino's tonight?
    B. _____

4. A. Thank you very much for all your help.
    B. _____

5. A. Oh wow! What a great room. It's wonderful.
    B. _____

6. A. We'd better leave now – our train leaves in half an hour.

    B. _____

7. A. It's been nice seeing you again. Let's get together again soon.
    B. _____

8. A. Hi, Tom. How are you?
    B. _____

9. A. Do you mind if I smoke in here?
    B. _____

10. A. I didn't do too well in the end of semester exams.
    B. _____

11. A. Have you ever heard of the Darwin Awards?
    B. _____

12. A. Do you think you'll do well in tomorrow's test?
    B. _____

Exercise 3
Instructions as above.

Have a good time. • How's it going? • Oh well, it's not the end of the world. • I'll say.
Gesundheit! • Not on your life! • Of course. Take a seat.
So I guess you're in the doghouse again. • Sure thing. • That's a load off my mind.
Well, keep it to yourself. • Well, take it easy. Don't kill yourself.

1. A. I'm about halfway through my essay.
    B. _____

2. A. I thought the lecture on the Declaration of Independence was great. Did you enjoy it?
    B. _____

3. A. Snake is considered a delicacy in some countries. Would you ever consider eating it?
    B. _____

4. A. Professor de Gruchy has extended the deadline for our essays to Thursday, so you don't need to worry about not finishing it on time.
    B. _____

5. A. Did you know that our economics teacher has left the questions for tomorrow's test lying on his desk?
    B. _____

6. A. Could you give me a bit of help with this assignment?
    B. _____

7. A. Can I come in?
    B. _____

8. A. I have so much to do by Monday; two essays to write, a presentation to prepare, and I have to do some research on the history of the U.N.
    B. _____

9. A. I'm so depressed. That's the third time I've failed my driver's test.
    B. _____

10. A. I'm off to Niagara Falls for the weekend. See you Monday.
    B. _____

11. A. I forgot my boyfriend's birthday last week.
    B. _____

12. A. Aaachoooooooo!
    B. _____

Idioms and colloquialisms 3

Connect the first part of each sentence in the first box on this page with the second half in the second box on the next page. Use the expressions in **bold** to help you make the connection.

1. If you come late, could you please **let me**…

2. I was rather unhappy when she **made a**…

3. The project was **more or**…

4. I just need to complete this essay, and then my coursework will be over **once and**…

5. His lectures are generally really dull, but **once in**…

6. I've never been **too**…

7. There are parts of the course which are a bit boring, but **on the**…

8. Don't try to do everything at once. Try to do things **step by**…

9. There's a chance that **sooner or**…

10. When you first start a new job, it can take a while to **learn the**…

11. I know you have a lot of work, but **look on the bright** …

12. The President can't be **in his right**…

13. You shouldn't **go over his**…

14. You're kidding. You're **pulling my**…

15. It can be difficult to **make ends**…

16. Try to **make the most of your**…

17. I asked Ron to get the computer fixed, and he promised to **take**…

18. I understand the theory, but I **get mixed**…

19. Don't worry about the exam. Just **give it**…

20. I'm not sure whether to take a vacation this summer. I'll decide **one way or**…

21. I wasn't sure whether to apply for a Ph.D. course, but in the end I decided to **go**…

22. I got a grade A for my first assignment of the year. That's **a good**…

23. For years he was ignored, then **all at**…

24. Many people believe that it's **about**…

25. I've **changed**…

26. He had some excellent plans, but they never really **got off**…

A.	...**big** on science; I've always preferred the arts.
B.	...**the ground**.
C.	...**whole** it's really good.
D.	...**start**, isn't it?
E.	...**all you've got** and hope for the best.
F.	...**for all**. It'll be a real relief.
G.	...**mind**, making a stupid decision like that.
H.	...**step** until you've finished.
I.	...**up** when I try to describe it on paper.
J.	...**the other** when I see my exam results.
K.	...**care of** it at the earliest opportunity.
L.	...**leg**. Right?
M.	...**my mind** about attending Professor Malkovich's course.
N.	...**for it** and see what happens.
O.	...**meet** when you're a student on a low income.
P.	...**later** the students will demand some real changes.
Q.	...**ropes** and become familiar with the way things work.
R.	...**head** and make your own decisions.
S.	...**point of** reminding me about my previous bad grades.
T.	...**less** complete when someone pointed out they had missed some details.
U.	...**know** in advance.
V.	...**time** when you're in New York.
W.	...**side**; at least you won't get bored this weekend!
X.	...**a while** there's something of interest.
Y.	...**time** more money was invested in education.
Z.	...**once**, people began paying attention to what he had to say.

Idioms and colloquialisms 4

Exercise 1
Choose the correct underlined word to complete each of the idioms in **bold**. The meaning of each idiom is in brackets after the sentence.

1.   You shouldn't try to **burn the match / lighter / candle** at both ends; you'll exhaust yourself. (*to get up early in the morning and go to bed late at night on a regular basis*)

2.   Once he started looking into the details, he realized what **a can of worms / beans / beer** they were opening. (*a difficult and complicated situation*)

3.   It was a difficult decision, but he decided to **take the goat / cow / bull by the horns** and tell his boss that he wanted to leave the company. (*to deal bravely or confidently with a difficult situation*)

4.   Some insurance companies make their customers **pay through the ears / nose / mouth** for their services. (*to pay a lot of money*)

5.   He knew that what they were doing was wrong, but **turned a blind / closed / cold eye** to it. (*to pretend not to notice, to ignore*)

6.   Many people like to get **off the beaten road / path / track** when they take a vacation. (*somewhere quiet, where not a lot of people go*)

7.   If you're **pressed / crushed / squeezed for time**, we can talk later. (*busy, in a hurry*)

8.   I've been feeling a bit **under the thumb / weather / table** recently, but I'm feeling better now. (*slightly sick*)

9.   He's a rather boring person, but **once in a blue / red / green moon**, he'll come out with something really amazing. (*very rarely*)

10.   I'm afraid your request is **out of the answer / statement / question**. (*not possible, unacceptable*)

11.   He gave us some information that was strictly **off the books / record / list**. (*unofficial, to be kept secret*)

12.   We don't want to **lose land / ground / place** in the baseball competition. (*to become less successful than the others*)

13.   Let's have a party at the beginning of the year. It will help to **break the ice / mold / air**. (*to make people feel more friendly and willing to talk to each other*)

14.   Everybody should say exactly how they feel. That should **clear the room / air / feelings**. (*to help end an argument or disagreement*)

15.   It's very rude to **talk shop / work / jobs** when you're out with other people. (*to discuss your job with a coworker, usually in a social situation where there are others present*)

16.   Don't let him stop you; **stand your land / place / ground** and tell him you won't change your mind. (*to refuse to change your mind about something, even when people oppose you*)

17.   I only just passed my exam. It was a very **far / close / exact thing**. (*something almost did or didn't happen*)

18.   What's happened? **Put me in the picture / story / scene**. (*to let somebody know what has happened, usually when other people already know*)

Exercise 2
Instructions as above.

1. You've really **made a <u>name</u> / title / place for yourself**, haven't you? (*to become well known, famous and / or respected*)

2. Have you seen his house? It's **out of this planet / earth / <u>world</u>**. (*extremely good, wonderful, etc.*)

3. He knew I was friendly with his boss, and asked me to **pull a few legs / <u>strings</u> / ropes** for him. (*to use your influence with somebody in order to get something*)

4. Donna **played / did / <u>went</u> hooky** again today; that's the third lecture she's missed this week. (*to miss a lesson, class, etc., for no good reason*)

5. My bank account's **in the black / <u>red</u> / pink** again. (*to owe money to the bank because you've spent too much*)

6. I've completed three out of my five essays already. **So far, so <u>good</u> / fine / acceptable**. (*until now, everything is going well*)

7. I'm really angry with Jerry. It's time I **had it <u>in</u> / out / over with** him. (*to tell somebody you are angry with them, and explain why*)

8. His theories **broke fresh earth / <u>ground</u> / land** and changed the way people thought about science. (*to do something original or innovative*)

9. He said that he had missed his lecture because he had to visit a sick relative, but I don't really think he was **on the air/ ground / <u>level</u>**. (*being honest and telling the truth*)

10. It wasn't my fault! Why am I always the one to **carry the <u>can</u> / tin / box**? (*being the person who is considered responsible for something that has gone wrong*)

11. University life can seem strange at first, but my advice is to **go with the snow / <u>flow</u> / glow** and see what happens. (*to do what seems the easiest thing in a particular situation*)

12. I thought my last essay was really good, so old Professor Clack really **rained on my show / carnival / <u>parade</u>** when he told me he thought it was terrible. (*to spoil something or make it much less enjoyable*)

13. The Dean has told me that unless I **turn over a new <u>leaf</u> / book / paper**, I might be asked to leave the course. (*to change your life by starting to be a better person or stopping a bad habit*)

14. There are some good restaurants nearby that **won't bankrupt / <u>break</u> / rob the bank**. (*not expensive*)

15. I can't talk to you now, I'm afraid. I'm **<u>running</u> / walking / jumping a bit late**. (*to be slightly later than normal*)

16. He can be a bit unfriendly, but **by and big / <u>large</u> / huge** he's OK. (*generally*)

17. All right, everyone. We've achieved a lot in the last hour or so. Let's **take three / four / <u>five</u>**. (*to have a short break*)

18. I don't know exactly what he's up to, but my **fifth / <u>sixth</u> / seventh sense** tells me he trying to get out of doing his assignment. (*a special ability to feel things that you cannot see, hear, touch, smell, or taste*)

Metaphor

A metaphor is a word or phrase that means one thing and is used to refer to another thing in order to emphasize their similar qualities. For example, in the sentence *"Picasso was the father of the Cubist movement"*, the word *father* is not used in its usual sense to mean someone's male parent. It means that Picasso was the person who started the Cubist movement, or that he was the first one to do it successfully. *Father* is being used in a *metaphorical* way. Metaphors are a bit like idioms (see pages 15 – 22), because the words and expressions are not being used with their literal meaning.

The following exercises look at some common metaphors that are used in different situations.

Exercise 1: achievements, ideas, and theories
Metaphorically, achievements, ideas, and theories are often seen as buildings, with an idea or the process of achieving something being similar to the process of building, and the failure of something being similar to the destruction of a building. Metaphorically, ideas are also like plants, and developing an idea is like getting plants to grow.
Complete sentences 1 – 20 with a word or expression from the box. In several cases you will need to change the form of the words. The first one has been done for you.

architect blueprint build on build up buttress collapse construct deep-rooted
demolish edifice fertile fruitful ground-breaking lay the foundations ruins
sow the seeds stem from take root towering under construction

1. The newspaper article threatened the whole _____*edifice*_____ of government, from the President all the way down to grass-roots politicians.

2. The company directors were convinced people would want their new product, but then early research and negative feedback began to _____ of doubt in their minds.

3. His argument was carefully _____ and was extremely difficult to dispute.

4. Her ideas were carefully _____ by a series of results showing that they had been put into practice and actually worked.

5. Superstitious beliefs are _____ in many cultures, and nothing can change these beliefs.

6. He was the chief _____ of the country's new economic policies.

7. The new government _____ for radical changes to the voting system, all of which would be implemented over the next five years.

8. The invention of the microchip was a _____ achievement.

9. The contract acted as a _____ for future cooperation between the two organizations.

10. The business was started in 1986, and over the next 20 years was _____ into one of the most powerful companies in the country.

11. The new constitution was _____ traditional values and a desire for progress.

12. The website is _____, but we hope to have it up and running by the end of the month.

13.   The idea seemed good in theory, but _____ when practical tests were first carried out.

14.   The new technology was revolutionary and _____, but was initially seen as a simple novelty.

15.   His life's work was in _____, but it did not deter him from starting again.

16.   I put forward several ideas, but to my anger and disappointment each one was comprehensively _____ by the board.

17.   His books were very popular because he had a _____ imagination and a talent for telling a good story.

18.   Nobody believed him at first, but a series of unexplained events meant that his ideas quickly _____ and people were more prepared to listen to him.

19.   Her ideas _____ her belief in the existence of life on other planets.

20.   The discussion was very _____, and we all came away from it believing that at last we were going to achieve something worthwhile.

Exercise 2: Other metaphors.

Look at sentences A, B, and C in the following groups, and look especially at the words and expressions in **bold**. Then rearrange the letters in italics in the final sentence to make another word or words. The final sentence should then explain what the metaphors in the first three sentences are describing. Note that two of the final sentences use the same word. The first one has been done as an example.

1.   (A) Your point of view is **indefensible**.
        (B) There was a lot of **conflict** over what to do next.
        (C) The team **clashed** over what steps to take next.

        Metaphorically, an *muntrage* is like a fight or a war, with people "attacking" and "defending".
        (Answer = *argument*)

2.   (A) She was one of the **brightest** students in the class.
        (B) As a child, Einstein was believed to have a rather **dull** mind.
        (C) She had a sudden **flash** of inspiration and began writing down her thoughts.

        Metaphorically, *ngeelcneilti* is like a light. The more you have, the brighter the light is.

3.   (A) I was wondering if I could rely on your **support**.
        (B) Would you mind **lending** me a **hand** with my assignment?
        (C) The government helped to **prop up** the college by offering it a financial grant.

        Metaphorically, when you *sitsas* someone, it is like supporting them physically (for example, with your body).

4.   (A) He is often regarded as the **greatest** writer of the twentieth century.
        (B) Everyone agreed that there were some **weighty** issues to be discussed at the meeting.
        (C) The novel received some good reviews, but many people thought it was rather **lightweight**.

        Metaphorically, something that is *taprmotni* is like something that is big or heavy, and something that is *ntaprmotniu* is small or light.

5.   (A) They only succeeded by using their political **muscle**.
        (B) She didn't have the **backbone** to accept his challenge.
        (C) I know it's difficult, but you have to **put your back into** it if you want to succeed.

        Metaphorically, making an *trofef* is like using a part of your body.

6.   (A) You look confused: let me **throw some light on** the matter.
        (B) Her work greatly **illuminated** this aspect of the subject.
        (C) I don't want to be **kept in the dark**, so please let me know what is happening.

Metaphorically, when you have *gwednloke* about something, it is like shining a light on it (and when you lack this, it is like being in darkness).

7.　(A) His new career **opened the door** to a whole new way of life.
　　(B) Having a University degree is arguably the **key** to success in life.
　　(C) Age should be **no barrier** to success.

Metaphorically, having the *roitpoytupn* to do something is like having a door or other entrance opened for you.

8.　(A) We **unearthed** some useful facts and figures.
　　(B) Her latest book is a **goldmine** of useful information.
　　(C) We **left no stone unturned** in our search for the truth.

Metaphorically, when you *oeidrvsc* things such as facts and information, it is similar to finding them by digging or searching in the ground.

9.　(A) He originally **set out** to become a priest, but became involved in politics instead.
　　(B) At the age of 24, things **took an unexpected turn** for him.
　　(C) After six years in the same job, I decided to **move on**.

Metaphorically, a *ilef* or *raecer* path is like a journey.

10.　(A) They put a lot of **pressure** on him to make change his mind.
　　(B) The country was **dragged** reluctantly into war.
　　(C) I'm sorry to **press** you for an answer, but we need to know your plans.

Metaphorically, when you *ecfro* someone to do something, it is like putting physical pressure on them (for example, by pulling or pushing them).

11.　(A) He was very **sharp-witted** and could always be relied on to come up with an astute comment when asked.
　　(B) She has a **keen** intellect and makes sure that everyone knows it.
　　(C) He was an **incisive** critic who always researched his subject thoroughly before passing comment on it.

Metaphorically, *eengintecill* is like a knife, a blade, or another sharp object.

12.　(A) We **covered a lot of ground** at the meeting.
　　(B) I'd like to **return** to the point I was making earlier.
　　(C) After three hours, we finally **arrived** at a decision.

Metaphorically, a *veoantcirosn* or *nosisidscu* is like a journey, with the people who are speaking going from one place to another.

13.　(A) We need to address the social **ills** that are at the root of crime.
　　(B) The country was **paralyzed** by a series of natural and man-made disasters.
　　(C) Drugs such as heroin and cocaine are seen as a **cancer** at the very heart of society.

Metaphorically, a *beprmol* is like an illness.

14.　(A) The speaker received a very **warm** welcome from the audience.
　　(B) We had several good ideas, but they **poured cold water** on all of them.
　　(C) I was disappointed because his response was rather **lukewarm**.

Metaphorically, *anesismuht* and *nicetxetem* are like heat, and a lack of these is like cold or wet.

15.　(A) The biography mainly dealt with his years **at the top**.
　　(B) Many people commented on his rapid **ascent up the ladder**.
　　(C) His greed and lack of integrity eventually led to his **downfall**.

Metaphorically, being *fucsuscsel* is like being high up, and *uraelfi* is like falling or being low down.

Numbers and symbols

How do you say the numbers and symbols in **bold** in these sentences?

1. **2006** was the company's most profitable year since **1994**.

2. The advantage of Internet banking is that you can check your account **24/7**.

3. Despite a rigorous advertising campaign, demand has only risen by **0.8**% in the last two months.

4. We're meeting in his office at **3:45** this afternoon.

5. Your flight for Zurich leaves at **1800** from Logan International Airport.

6. I expect to be back in the country on **June 30**.

7. Our next range of products will be released on **10/3**.

8. She completed the test in a record **27½** minutes.

9. **¾** of all our employees think the canteen food could be improved.

10. The new desk measures exactly **6ft.** x **3ft.** x **3ft.**

11. Is this printer really only **$1.99**?

12. Oh, sorry sir, that's a mistake. The sticker should say **$100.99**.

13. And that computer doesn't cost **$120.75**. It actually costs **$1120.75**.

14. Please quote reference **ACB81 - 25/B**.

15. Our new telephone number is **(212) 909-7940**.

16. For more information, call **1-800-528-4800**.

17. Alternatively, ring **1-800-AXP-1234**.

18. The emergency telephone number in the U.S.A. is **911**. In the U.K. it's **999**. In Australia it's **000**.

19. To access the information you require, press the **#** key, followed by the **0** key, and finally the ***** key.

20. He earns a salary of over **$200K** a year! In fact, he's making so much money that he plans to retire in his **mid-50's**.

21. We have invested over **$6M** in new technology.

22. The union held a ballot to see if the workers wanted to strike. The result was **2:1** in favor.

23. My email address is markbarrington**@snailmail.com**.

24. Hi Todd. **GR8** news on the promotion. I'm really **:-)** for you! **CUL8R** for a celebratory drink?

25. He drives to work in a big, fuel-guzzling **4x4**.

26. The Denver Deadbeats won the match against the Washington Washouts by **2:0**. In the game against the Los Angeles Layabouts the following week, they tied **3:3**.

27. At the last census, the population of the country was **37,762,418**.

28. It's important to send your **1099** form to the IRS on time.

29. This book is **©** Rawdon Wyatt, 2007.

30. The "Ultimafone**®**" has just won a "Product of the Year" award.

Obligation and option

Complete sentences 1 – 17 with a suitable word from the box. More than one answer is possible in some cases.

alternative	compelled	compulsory	entail	essential	exempt	forced	have	liable
mandatory	must	need	obligation	obliged	optional	require	voluntary		

1.   A valid passport and visa are _____ by all visitors to the country. Unless you have these, you will not be allowed in.

2.   Attendance at all classes is _____. You may not miss a class without prior arrangement with your course leader.

3.   Note to new students: all fees _____ be paid no later than one week before the commencement of the course. Your place on the course may be forfeited if you fail to satisfy this requirement.

4.   Before you make an appointment with the college doctor, you _____ to register your name at the clinic, which you will find in the Administrative Block.

5.   If you cause any damage to property, whether accidentally or on purpose, you will be held _____ for any costs incurred.

6.   The college was _____ to refund part of its student fees after they announced that several of the course modules would no longer be running.

7.   Books, clothes, and food are currently _____ from government tax, as they are considered necessities rather than luxuries.

8.   _____ police security checks are carried out on all students and members of staff who will be working or associating with minors (i.e., those under 18).

9.   Entrance to the museum is free, but visitors are asked to make a _____ donation of $5.

10.   Evening lectures and presentations are _____: it is up to you whether you attend or not.

11.   Unless your attendance improves, the college will have no _____ but to ask you to leave the course.

12.   Manufacturers of packaged foods are _____ to list all the ingredients contained clearly on the box or package. This should include any artificial colorings and additives.

13.   You are under no _____ to work overtime, but we hope that you would be prepared to work late at least once a week.

14.   When Professor Ranscombe was accused of making sexist remarks in his lectures, he felt _____ to write a public letter of apology to those he had offended.

15.   The project is very exciting, but everyone realizes that it will _____ a lot of work.

16.   There's no _____ to make an appointment to see me. Just turn up at my office anytime after lunch.

17.   It is absolutely _____ that the two liquids are kept separate, otherwise a chemical reaction could trigger an explosion.

Opinion, attitude, and belief

Rearrange the letters in **bold** in the following sentences to make words that can be used to talk about opinion, attitude, and belief. The first letter of each word has been underlined for you. Write these words in the appropriate space in the grid that follows the sentences. If you do this correctly, you will reveal a word in the shaded vertical strip that means "not willing to accept much change, especially in the traditional values of society". This word can be used to complete sentence 13.

1.   As far as I am **enodccenr**, happiness is more important than money.

2.   In my **nponioi**, technology is moving too quickly.

3.   She **aitainsmn** that most young people would rather work than go to school.

4.   We strongly **pesctus** that the proposal to develop the computer facilities will not go ahead.

5.   I take strong **etonepixc** to people coming late or cancelling appointments at short notice.

6.   The government are **ingerdgar** the debt that is owed by developing nations as a major barrier to global economic progress.

7.   Scientists are **cdnoevcin** that human degradation of the environment is causing thousands of species to become extinct.

8.   A lot of people are **atifalnac** about sport in general and football in particular.

9.   I **butdo** that the new government will keep all its promises.

10.   They come from a strongly **taitoanrdil** family who still believe in arranged marriages.

11.   Do you **popvisread** of smoking?

12.   The government are **micedtomt** to the struggle to end institutional racism in the police force.

Use the word in the shaded vertical strip to complete this sentence:

13.   He has very _____ views and disapproves of change.

1.															
2.															
3.															
4.															
5.															
6.															
7.															
8.															
9.															
10.															
11.															
12.															

Exercise 2
Hidden in the box on the next page you will find 40 more words related to opinion, attitude, and belief. These words can be found by reading from left to right and from top to bottom only. Find these words and then use them to complete definitions 1 – 40.

```
Q  M  I  D  D  L  E  O  F  T  H  E  R  O  A  D  W  S  E  R  T  Y
P  U  S  I  O  I  N  T  E  L  L  E  C  T  U  A  L  I  P  R  A  S  S
R  D  O  G  V  E  G  A  N  T  O  L  E  R  A  N  T  K  B  O  F  S
A  G  C  A  P  I  T  A  L  I  S  M  J  E  W  A  H  H  I  Y  J  U
G  O  I  C  H  R  I  S  T  I  A  N  I  T  Y  R  K  I  G  A  L  P
M  P  A  D  Z  X  D  E  M  O  C  R  A  T  C  C  V  S  O  L  B  E
A  I  L  I  V  E  G  E  T  A  R  I  A  N  B  H  N  M  T  I  U  R
T  N  I  M  U  S  L  I  M  M  Q  W  R  A  C  I  S  T  E  S  D  S
I  I  S  T  A  T  H  E  I  S  T  E  R  H  T  S  Y  U  D  T  D  T
C  O  M  M  U  N  I  S  M  I  C  H  R  I  S  T  I  A  N  O  H  I
P  N  A  S  A  G  N  O  S  T  I  C  D  N  T  A  O  I  S  M  I  T
M  A  F  G  J  U  D  A  I  S  M  M  O  D  E  R  A  T  E  S  S  I
O  T  J  R  E  P  U  B  L  I  C  A  N  U  K  C  Y  N  I  C  M  O
R  E  E  G  A  L  I  T  A  R  I  A  N  S  T  O  I  C  A  L  L  U
A  D  O  B  S  E  S  S  I  V  E  O  P  E  N  M  I  N  D  E  D  S
L  X  I  S  L  A  M  C  D  O  G  M  A  T  I  C  V  B  N  M  Q  W
E  P  A  C  I  F  I  S  T  R  T  Y  U  F  A  S  C  I  S  M  C  A
```

1. Someone who is well educated and interested in art, science, literature, etc., at a high level: an _____.

2. Someone who believes that their country should have a king or queen: a _____.

3. A political system that aims to create a society in which everyone has equal opportunities and in which the most important industries are owned or controlled by the whole community: _____.

4. An economic system in which property, businesses, and industry are owned by individual people and not by the government: _____.

5. A political and economic system is which there is no private ownership of property and industry and in which people of all social classes are treated equally: _____.

6. Someone who chooses not to eat anything made from, or produced by, animals, including fish, eggs, milk, cheese, and honey: a _____.

7. Someone who chooses not to eat meat or fish: a _____.

8. An adjective describing someone who thinks about something all the time because they think it is extremely important, even if it is not, and even if other people believe they are thinking about it too much: _____.

9. A four-word adjective describing opinions, attitudes, styles, etc., which are not extreme: _____.

10. An adjective describing people who are willing to accept other people's beliefs, way of life, etc., without criticizing them (even if they disagree with them): _____.

11. An adjective relating to right and wrong and the way people should behave. It can be used to describe people who base their actions on what they believe rather than what rules or laws say is right: _____.

12. Someone who does not like or respect people who belong to races that are different from their own, and who thinks their race is better than others: a _____.

13. A two word adjective describing someone who is willing to consider new ideas: _____.

14. An adjective describing someone who is so sure that their beliefs and ideas are right that they expect other people to accept them: _____.

15. Someone who believes that there should be no governments or laws: an _____.

16. An adjective describing someone who accepts bad things without complaining: _____.

17. An adjective describing someone who has opinions that most people think are unreasonable, especially about race, politics, and religion: _____.

18. An adjective to describe someone who bases their actions on achieving practical results rather than on theories and ideas: _____.

19. Someone whose opinions and actions are reasonable and not extreme, especially in politics: a _____.

20. An adjective to describe someone who has very strong opinions that they refuse to change, even when they are clearly unreasonable: _____.

21. In the U.S.A., a political party whose members usually have conservative views. Elsewhere, someone who believes that a government should have a president and representatives elected by the people: _____.

22. In the U.S.A., a member of the political party (with the same name) whose policies are usually more liberal than those of number 21 above. Elsewhere, someone who supports democracy as a political system: a _____.

23. The religion based on the ideas of the prophet Muhammad: _____.

24. Someone who is a follower of the religion in number 23 above: a _____.

25. The religion based on the ideas of Jesus Christ: _____.

26. Someone who is a follower of the religion in number 25 above: _____.

27. The religion based on the writings of the *Torah* and the *Talmud*: _____.

28. Someone who is a follower of the religion in number 27 above: a _____.

29. The main religion of India, which believes in reincarnation: _____.

30. Someone who is a follower of the religion in number 29 above: a _____.

31. The Indian religious group that separated from number 29 above in the 16th century: _____.

32. The set of religious beliefs based on the teachings of Siddharta Gautama: _____.

33. A Chinese system of religion and thought that says people should live a simple, natural, and honest life: _____.

34. An adjective used to describe a person, society, etc., that believes that everyone is equal and should have the same rights: _____.

35. A very right-wing political system in which the government is very powerful and controls the society and economy completely without allowing any opposition: _____.

36. Someone who does not believe in the existence of God: an _____.

37. Someone who believes that it is not possible to know whether God exists or not: an _____.

38. Someone who believes that people care only about themselves and are not sincere or honest: a _____.

39. Someone who believes that violence is wrong and refuses to fight in or support wars: a _____.

40. An adjective describing someone who believes in the power of magic or luck: _____.

Opposites: Verbs

Replace the verbs in **bold** in sentences 1 – 26 with a word or expression from the box which has an opposite meaning in the same context. In many cases you will need to change the form of the word (for example, to its past simple form).

abandon	abolish	attack	conceal	decline	demolish	deny	deteriorate	exaggerate
extend	fall	forbid	gain	hire	lend	loosen	lower	postpone	refuse
reject	replenish	reward	set	simplify	succeed	withdraw		

1. They **accepted** the offer of a ceasefire.

2. He **admitted** telling lies in his original statement.

3. They **agreed** to meet to discuss the future of the organization.

4. The senator **defended** his opponent's policies in a televised speech.

5. The apartments blocks they **built** were the ugliest in the city.

6. He **complicated** matters by rewriting the original proposal.

7. They **continued** their plans to assassinate the king when he opened Parliament.

8. He **deposited** $10,000 – half his college fees for the forthcoming year.

9. Relations between the two countries have **improved** considerably in the last year.

10. He **permitted** us to present our petition directly to the President.

11. The members of the commune were **punished** for their part in the revolution.

12. He **raised** the overall standards of the company within two months of his appointment.

13. As soon as the sun **rose**, the demonstrators began to appear on the streets.

14. Prices **rose** sharply in the first three months of the financial year.

15. As soon as he had **tightened** the knots, he pushed the boat out.

16. To everyone's surprise, she **failed**.

17. Tomorrow's meeting has been **brought forward**.

18. The management said that they would be happy to **borrow** the money.

19. Several flaws in the design of the new model were **revealed**.

20. The course has been **shortened** to 12 weeks.

21. I don't want to **underestimate** his role in the club.

22. Attendance has **increased** since the new professor took over the course.

23. Fuel supplies have been **exhausted**.

24. Despite having a bigger and cheaper choice of healthy foods, many Americans have **lost** a lot of weight.

25. Following the revolution, the monarchy was **restored**.

26. The company started seeing some success once they **dismissed** several employees.

Exercise 2

Some verbs can be made into their opposite form, or otherwise modified, by the addition of the prefixes *dis-*, *im-*, *mis-*, or *un-*.

In each of the sentences below, change the verb in bold into its opposite form using one of the prefixes above. In most cases, you should also need to change the end of the verb (by adding *-s*, *-ed*, *-ing*, etc., and in some cases by also removing a letter). Then use your answers to complete the crossword on the next page.

Across (⇩)

2. The press have once again **quote** the President: he said that women were "America's hope for the future", and not "America's hopeless future".

3. The National Patients' Association is calling on Senators around the country to make doctors legally responsible for **diagnose** an illness.

6. Despite recent rumors in the press, Kaput Computers is pleased to announce that it will *not* be **continue** its popular range of discounted computers for students.

8. The press deliberately tried to **represent** our college, wrongly suggesting that we only recruit students whose parents make large financial donations to the college.

10. Once the film has been **load** from the camera, it needs to kept in a dark, dry place until it can be processed.

12. If any students **agree** with the new regulations, they should put their concerns in a letter to the Course Director.

13. If any student **use** the college computers (e.g., for accessing undesirable websites), they will be instantly suspended.

14. In his new book "Stars in my Eyes", astronomer Harvey Weiss claims to **lock** the secrets of the universe.

16. As the full extent of the disaster **fold**, the government decided to take drastic action.

20. Employers have every right to **trust** interview candidates who are not able to provide adequate references or show proof of their qualifications.

22. The college staff **approve** of students smoking on the premises.

23. He was surprised that everyone had **obey** the rules.

Down (⇨)

1. We completely **judge** the time we had for the project, and unfortunately we were unable to finish on time.

2. When one group of people **understand** another, usually as a result of linguistic or cultural differences, physical conflict is often the result.

4. Before **connect** the copier from the power supply, make sure it is switched off.

5. Students who are caught cheating will be immediately **qualify**.

7. Your lack of progress on this course has **please** your tutor, and in view of this he plans report you to the Principal.

9. I accidentally **calculate** the amount we needed to spend on fees and accommodations.

11. It is a sad fact of college life that unless some students are properly supervised, they will take every opportunity to **behave**.

15. We claimed $20,000 for fire damage, but the claim was **allow** because we hadn't observed proper safety procedures.

17. We regret that our trust in you was sadly **place**, and therefore we will not be dealing with you in the future.

18. A recent investigation has **cover** several cases of unauthorized Internet use in the library.

19. The huge increase in exports recently has **prove** the argument that the world has stopped buying American goods.

21. Unfortunately, but not surprisingly, many of our students **like** the increased workload this semester.

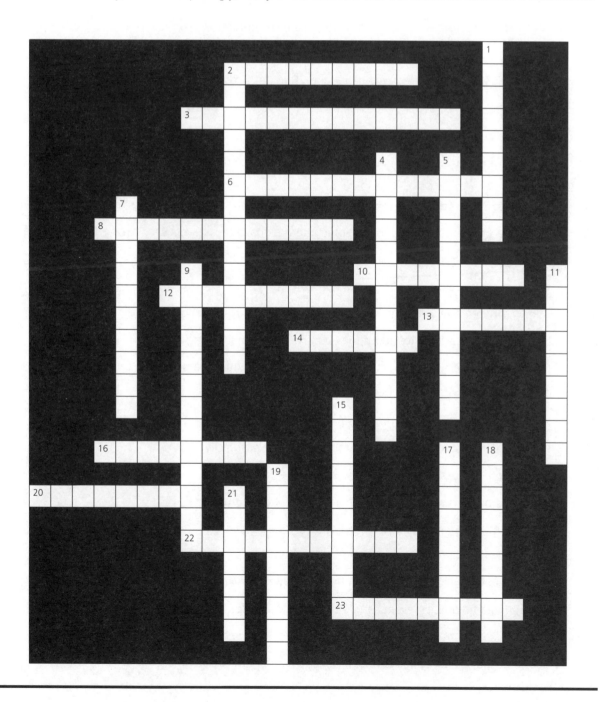

Opposites: Adjectives

Replace the adjectives in **bold** in sentences 1 – 28 with a word or expression from the box which has an opposite meaning in the same context.

approximate	archaic	artificial	clear	commonplace	compulsory	considerable	crude
delicate	detrimental	dim	easy	even	feasible	flexible	graceful	innocent	intricate
negligible	problematic	scarce	smooth	reluctant	spontaneous	tedious	vibrant
		worthless	worthwhile				

1. The meaning of his words was very **ambiguous**.

2. According to his colleagues, he's a very **awkward** person to deal with.

3. When she first started dancing, she was very **awkward**.

4. His policies were **beneficial** to the economy as a whole.

5. We need **exact** figures before we embark on a new venture.

6. The jury decided he was **guilty** of the crime.

7. Add up all the **odd** numbers between 1 and 20 to get a result.

8. Despite the weather, supplies of food after the harvest were **plentiful**.

9. The laws restricting pollution in the city are very **rigid**.

10. There is a **slight** difference in the way the company is run these days compared with a few years ago.

11. The device is very **sophisticated** and should only be operated by someone who is familiar with it.

12. The spices used in the production of some international dishes have a very **strong** flavor.

13. The **bright** light from the flashlight picked out details on the walls of the cave.

14. Attendance at afternoon classes should be **voluntary**.

15. A lot of students are **willing** to attend classes on Saturday morning.

16. Newspapers are saying a lot about the country's **modern** licensing laws.

17. Many students believe that doing voluntary work for charities is a **pointless** cause.

18. The country displayed all the features of a **stagnant** economy.

19. Her lectures are extremely **interesting**.

20. **Planned** demonstrations and strikes took place all over the city.

21. The plans they presented were **simple** and well written.

22. A close study of the painting by experts revealed it to be **priceless**.

23. The new rules had a **profound** impact on everyone's behavior.

24. What you are asking me to do is quite **impossible**.

25. Contrary to what many people think, this is a very **rare** event.

26. Organizing a fundraising event can be surprisingly **simple**.

27. From a distance, the surface of the planet appears to be very **rough**.

28. The confectionery contained several flavors, all of them **natural**.

Exercise 2

A lot of adjectives can be made into their opposite form by adding a *prefix* (*un-*, *in-*, *dis-*, *il-*, etc.) to the beginning of the word.

Task 1: Decide which of the prefixes from the first box can be used to make opposites of the words in the second box.

dis-	il-	im-	in-	ir-	un-

acceptable	accurate	adequate	advantaged	agreeable	attractive
authorized	avoidable	believable	certain	comfortable	competent
complete	conscious	contented	convincing	correct	curable	even
fair	fashionable	honest	inclined	legal	limited	literate	logical
married	mature	moral	mortal	obedient	organized	patient
perfect	personal	possible	proper	pure	qualified	rational
regular	relevant	replaceable	resistible	resolute	responsible
satisfactory	satisfied	sufficient	welcome

Task 2: Without looking at your answers to Task 1, look at the following sentences and paragraphs. In each one there is one word which has been given the wrong prefix. Decide which word is wrong and correct it.

1. He is a very (A) <u>disagreeable</u> man and he makes visitors feel very (B) <u>unwelcome</u>, but the management think he's (C) <u>irreplaceable</u> and are (D) <u>uninclined</u> to fire him.

2. Insider dealing is not only (A) <u>immoral</u> and (B) <u>inhonest</u>, but also (C) <u>illegal</u>: companies are legally bound to take the strongest possible action against such (D) <u>unacceptable</u> behavior by their employees.

3. It is an (A) <u>unavoidable</u> fact, but in a competitive job market, those who are (B) <u>unqualified</u> or who have (C) <u>imsufficient</u> work experience will find themselves seriously (D) <u>disadvantaged</u>.

4. She was described by her boss as being (A) <u>unresponsible</u>, (B) <u>incompetent</u>, and (C) <u>immature</u>, which she considered extremely (D) <u>unfair</u>.

5. In return for an increased investment, the company offered (A) <u>unlimited</u> returns for their investors. While many found such an offer (B) <u>irresistible</u>, some thought the promises were (C) <u>inconvincing</u> and were (D) <u>uncomfortable</u> about parting with so much money.

6. He had clearly given his presentation (A) <u>disadequate</u> preparation, and many in the audience challenged the points he made, saying they were (B) <u>inaccurate</u> and (C) <u>illogical</u>. Despite this, he remained (D) <u>irresolute</u> in his views, although the only person he managed to convince was himself.

Phrasal Verbs 1

Phrasal verbs are very common in English, and should be learnt like any other item of English vocabulary. In the TOEFL, they are tested in the Listening Comprehension section, and appear frequently in other parts of the test.

Exercise 1
In the following sentences, choose the correct verb in **bold** to complete the phrasal verb in *italics*. The meaning of each phrasal verb is given in brackets at the end of each sentence.

1. Some parents are criticized for the way they **bring** / **make** / **throw** *up* their children. (*to raise children*)

2. They refused to **move** / **face** / **come** *up to* their responsibilities, with disastrous consequences. (*to accept an unpleasant state of affairs, and try to deal with it*)

3. The President decided to **shout** / **cry** / **call** *off* his visit to Europe. (*to not to go ahead with a plan*)

4. It is only at election time that senators **add** / **count** / **read** *on* support from their constituents. (*to rely / depend on other people*)

5. Many developing countries are failing to **run** / **chase** / **catch** *up with* their more developed neighbors. (*to get to the same level*)

6. It can take months or even years for political scandals to **die** / **cut** / **fall** *down*. (*to become less strong*)

7. An alarming number of students **jump** / **drop** / **fall** *out of* school early every year. (*to leave a race, a competition, a course of study, etc., early or before you have finished*)

8. Major international companies can't **carry** / **cut** / **figure** *out* the popularity of the anti-capitalist movement. (*informal: to find it hard to understand*)

9. The committee members **dropped** / **made** / **fell** *out* over plans for the new health center. (*to argue*)

10. If they examined the issues more closely, they would **search** / **look** / **find** *out* the reasons. (*to discover*)

11. As we **grow** / **stand** / **look** *up* our priorities change. (*to change from being children to being adults*)

12. Salaries very rarely **catch** / **keep** / **work** *up with* the cost of living. (*to rise at the same speed as something else*)

13. The latest government report **leaves** / **keeps** / **throws** *out* the real reasons for current demographic shifts. (*to not include*)

14. The journalist **showed** / **pointed** / **spoke** *out* the mistakes made by the agency over the last few years. (*to show*)

15. Before you write your essay, you should **search** / **hunt** / **look** *into* the Party's history. (*to research*)

16. Nobody at the meeting **carried** / **brought** / **moved** *up* the subject of paid leave. (*to start discussing a subject*)

17. Once people **lose** / **jump** / **fall** *behind* with their mortgage payments, they come under extreme finascal pressure from their bank. (*to fail to do something or pay something at the time that you should*)

18. The first step to a healthier lifestyle is to **cut** / **slice** / **chop** *down* on the amount of saturated fats you eat. (*to start doing less of something, usually because it is bad for you*)

Exercise 2

Instructions as above. In one of the sentences, all of the verbs are possible.

1. During the early 2000's, a lot of state-run schools were **controlled** / **taken** / **acquired** over by private companies. (*to start to do something in place of someone else*)

2. In my last essay, I tried to **argue** / **place** / **put** forward the arguments in favor of global capitalism. (*to suggest or state the case for something*)

3. Despite the seriousness of the illness, he managed to **carry** / **pull** / **take** through. (*to recover from a serious illness or accident*)

4. A lot of restrictions on imports have been **done** / **gone** / **put** away with. (*to get rid of something*)

5. If you have a complaint, put it in writing and ask the company to **investigate** / **look** / **see** into it for you. (*to try to discover the facts about something such as a problem*)

6. It is very important to **carry** / **work** / **do** out my instructions carefully. (*to do something that you have been told to do, often in a particular way*)

7. Many employees **went** / **kept** / **carried** on working despite pressure from the unions. (*to continue*)

8. The drug's effects are very powerful, but they begin to **wear** / **come** / **fall** off after a few hours. (*to gradually disappear or become less intense*)

9. The meeting will be canceled if not enough people **arrive** / **move** / **turn** up. (*to come somewhere, often unexpectedly*)

10. At first, sales of the product were slow, but they **kicked** / **hit** / **picked** up when people realized how useful it was. (*to slowly improve*)

11. I have **given** / **put** / **moved** across several suggestions, but so far they have all been ignored. (*to explain an idea, often in a way that is easy for people to understand*)

12. I **came** / **ran** / **moved** into Laura outside the theater last week. (*to meet someone by chance*)

13. This course has **set** / **moved** / **put** me back by about $2000. (*informal: to cost someone a particular amount of money, especially a large amount*)

14. When I **look** / **consider** / **move** back on my childhood, I remember the many sacrifices my parents made for me. (*to think about something that happened in the past*)

15. We were all disappointed with the way things **turned** / **came** / **changed** out. (*to develop in a particular way or have a particular result*)

16. The exhibition was so popular that a lot of visitors had to be **pushed** / **turned** / **thrown** away. (*to be not allowed to enter a building*)

17. The total cost of the project **makes** / **moves** / **works** out to about $250,000. (*to add up to a particular amount*)

18. The telephone service is rather unreliable, and it's quite common to be **cut** / **shut** / **run** off in the middle of a conversation. (*to be disconnected while talking on the telephone*)

Phrasal Verbs 2

<u>Exercise 1</u>

Each of these sentences can be completed with *come*, *get*, *give*, *go*, or *look* to make a phrasal verb in **bold**. In some cases, more than one answer is possible. Make sure you use the correct form of the verb in each one. The phrasal verb is explained in brackets at the end of each sentence.

1.   In rural districts, it can be difficult to _____ **by** without a car. (*to work and operate efficiently*)

2.   I'd like you to _____ **over** these figures and tell me if you think the project is possible. (*to check something carefully*)

3.   Large industries can no longer _____ **away** with dumping industrial waste in rivers. (*to avoid being punished for doing something wrong or illegal*)

4.   Developed countries are usually able to _____ **through** a period of recession by drawing on financial reserves. (*to manage to deal with a difficult situation until it is over*)

5.   People who have to _____ **after** elderly relatives or other dependents should receive financial support. (*to take care of someone or something and make certain they have everything they need*)

6.   We decided to _____ **through** with our plans as soon as we had sufficient capital. (*to do something you have planned or agreed to do, especially after not being sure you wanted to do it*)

7.   It can be very difficult to _____ **down** to studying for exams when the weather is nice. (*to start doing something seriously or with a lot of effort*)

8.   Lights _____ **out** across the country as power workers went on strike. (*to stop burning or shining*)

9.   The committee were asked to _____ **into** the latest crime statistics and try to establish a pattern. (*to try to discover the facts about something such as a problem or crime*)

10.   After years of decline, government investment is revitalizing the area, and things are beginning to _____ **up**. (*to get better, or appear to get better*)

11.   Scientists _____ **across** the cure by accident, while studying the health benefits of a rare species of plant. (*to find something by chance*)

12.   Very few students _____ **forward** to their end-of-semester exams. (*to feel happy and excited about something that is going to happen*)

13.   Generally, people are reluctant to break unpopular rules, but will try to _____ **around** them somehow. (*to find a way of dealing with a problem or avoiding it*)

14.   The first step to a healthier lifestyle is to _____ **up** smoking. (*to stop doing something you do regularly*)

15.   The governor _____ **up against** a lot of opposition from locals when she proposed building a jail near the city limits. (*to have to deal with something difficult or unpleasant*)

16.   Even if you fail the first time, you should _____ **on** trying. (*to continue doing something*)

17.   The anti-smoking message is finally _____ **through to** people. (*to make someone understand what you are trying to say*)

18.   As ticket prices _____ **up**, fewer people go to the theater and prefer to stay at home with a video. (*to increase in price*)

Exercise 2
Instructions as above.

1. Doctors realized there was going to be a problem when several people in the same village _____ **down with** suspected food poisoning. (*to become ill with a particular disease*)

2. People often _____ **up** the idea of starting their own company when they realize the risks that are involved. (*to no longer want to do something*)

3. Before entering an agreement, it is essential to _____ **over** the details very carefully. (*to check something carefully*)

4. People who live in close proximity to one another must learn to _____ **along with** their neighbors. (*to try to like someone and be friendly to them*)

5. It was only after he _____ **into** his inheritance after his father died that he was able to expand the company. (*to receive money or property when someone dies*)

6. After the revolution, it took almost five years for the country to _____ **around to** opening its borders. (*to do something after you have intended to do it for some time*)

7. New legislation lays down strict penalties for vehicles which _____ **off** excess exhaust. (*to produce a gas or smell*)

8. People who want to know how to _____ **about** starting their own company should talk to a trained adviser. (*to start dealing with a situation, problem, job, etc., in a particular way*)

9. When supply of a particular good exceeds demand, it is common for the price to _____ **down**. (*to become cheaper*)

10. Nothing _____ **of** the company's plans to develop solar-powered vehicles. (*to be the result of something*)

11. The final bill for the project will _____ **to** almost $10 million. (*to reach a particular total when everything is added together*)

12. For most poor people, _____ **out of** the cycle of poverty can be next to impossible. (*to avoid or escape from an unpleasant situation*)

13. In any dispute with an insurance company, it is usually the consumer who _____ **off** the worst. (*to achieve a particular result in an activity, especially a competition, fight, or argument*)

14. It took a long time for the country to _____ **over** the effects of the civil war. (*to recover from something*)

15. The threat of severe reprisals meant that many refused to _____ themselves **up to** the police. (*to surrender to someone in a position of authority, especially to the police*)

16. Some people tend to _____ **down on** others who are less fortunate purely because of their financial situation. (*to think that you are better or more important than someone else*)

17. The government had decided to stand firm on their decision, but under pressure from protesters, they decided to _____ **in** and reduce tax on gasoline. (*to stop competing or arguing and accept that you cannot win*)

18. By the time the message _____ **through** it was too late to evacuate the residents. (*to be connected to someone by telephone, email, text message, etc.*)

Don't forget that many phrasal verbs can have more than one meaning. Try to develop your own written "bank" of the phrasal verbs you learn. This should show as many different meanings as possible for each phrasal verb. You should then try to remember these so that they become a part of your "productive" vocabulary.

Phrasal Verbs 3

• The verbs and particles in the two boxes below can be combined to make phrasal verbs, which can then be used to complete the sentences underneath.

• Decide which phrasal verbs go into each sentence, and write the answers in the crossword grid, which you will find on page 42. In many cases, you will need to change the form of the verb (e.g., past or present participle, third person "s", etc.). The meaning of each phrasal verb is in *italics* at the end of each sentence.

• Don't forget that some phrasal verbs need two particles.

• Do not put a gap between the verb and the particle(s) in the crossword grid.

add	break	bring	engage	factor
go	hand	hold	make	opt	pick
put	run	set	shut	stem
take	talk	turn		

about	after	against	apart	aside
down	for	from	in	into	of	off
on	out	round	to	up	with

Clues across (↧)

1. Accommodations in some cities are so expensive that some people cannot even afford to _____ the 8 weeks' deposit that is required. (*to make a deposit*)

5. They were reluctant to make changes, but we managed to _____ them _____. (*to persuade somebody*)

6. Children often _____ one of their parents, either in their mannerisms or in the way they look. (*to resemble*)

7. After _____ a few unexpected difficulties, they decided to scrap the project. (*to stop because something is in the way*)

9. When Mr. and Mrs. Johnson were unable to pay the rent on time, their landlord threatened to _____ them _____ onto the street. (*to force someone to leave*)

10. When I was at school, some teachers unfairly _____ children who eschewed sport for more creative interests and pastimes. (*to choose someone to attack or criticize*)

11. Although many companies offer their employees a pension plan, many decide to _____ of the program and make their own arrangements. (*to decide not to take part in something*)

16. A lot of applicants expressed an interest in the job, but only a handful _____ for the interview. (*to arrive for a meeting, appointment, etc.*)

19. Air pollution can _____ asthma and other chest diseases in those most vulnerable. (*to start*)

20. People who use credit cards unwisely can easily _____ debts of thousands of dollars every month. (*to make debts go up quickly*)

22. Parents often struggle to _____ enough money to pay for their children's education. (*to keep or save something from a larger amount in order to use it later for a particular purpose*)

24. The two men didn't _____ each other at first, but over the next year they became the best of friends. (*to begin to like someone or something*)

28. One of the best ways to get fit is to _____ a sport or activity. (*to start doing something regularly as a habit*)

30. The plans were _____ while we waited for a decision from the management. (*to cause a delay or make someone late*)

32.   The two sides are currently _____ talks which they hope will end the dispute. (*to take part in a particular activity, especially something that takes a lot of time and effort*)

36.   Her discovery _____ a chain of events that surprised everyone involved. (*to cause a situation or a series of events to happen*)

37.   After _____ expenditure and inflation, profits were very low. (*to include a particular amount when you calculate something*)

38.   Our money is _____ quickly, and if we don't act soon, it will be too late. (*to use all of something and not have any left*)

39.   Some students can be very creative with the reasons they give for not _____ their assignments on time. (*to give something to a person in authority*)

Clues down (⟲)

1.   It's often a good idea to _____ some money for a "rainy day". (*to save money*)

2.   Technology is moving at such a fast pace it is no longer possible to _____ all the latest developments. (*to understand or assimilate information*)

3.   Radical measures introduced by the college authorities did not _____ a genuine reform of the system. (*to combine to produce a particular result or effect*)

4.   Nobody was _____ by the government's false figures on unemployment. (*to be fooled or tricked*)

6.   He _____ the job that was offered to him, even though he was desperate for the money. (*to refuse something which is offered*)

8.   Most people will _____ a stressful job if the money is good enough. (*to tolerate something which is not very pleasant*)

12.   Once the equipment has been _____, it is surprisingly difficult to put it back together again. (*to separate an object into pieces*)

13.   The revolution was a long, bitter affair which _____ neighbor _____ neighbor. (*to cause two people or groups to fight each other, even though they were in a friendly relationship before*)

14.   Doctors and medical experts were unable to _____ why some people survived the virus and others didn't. (*to understand or know the reason for something*)

15.   Nobody believed the Senator's explanation for a moment. They all knew he had _____ it _____. (*to invent an explanation for something*)

17.   At the age of 38 he _____ the post of President, but lacked sufficient experience to be taken seriously. (*to apply for a job in politics, competing against other people for the same job*)

18.   Despite massive promotion by the tourist board, it took a long time for tourism to _____ again after the terrorist attacks. (*to improve, to get better*)

21.   Nothing can _____ the damage caused as a result of his actions. (*to take the place of something that has been lost or damaged, or to compensate for something bad that has happened*)

23.   The group plans to _____ an import business by the end of the year. (*to start something such as a business or organization*)

25.   The results of new rules will start to _____ next month, by which time we should all have familiarized ourselves with the system. (*informal: to start to have an effect*)

26.   His popularity _____ the fact that he was born in the area. (*to be caused by something*)

27.   The project will succeed unless someone decides to _____ at the last minute. (*to stop being involved in an activity, event or situation*)

29. For years women were _____ the political process. (*to not be allowed to do something or not be allowed to be involved in something*)

31. Major spending is required to _____ substantial improvement in housing. (*to make something happen, especially to cause changes in a situation*)

33. After several guests had _____ food poisoning, public health inspectors were called to the hotel. (*to become ill with a particular illness*)

34. It has always been my ambition to _____ show business. (*to start to have success in your career or an area of activity*)

35. At the auction, the painting _____ for an incredible $60 million. (*to be sold for a particular amount of money*)

Prefixes

Prefixes such as *dis-*, *im-*, *un-*, etc., can be used to make opposites of many verbs and adjectives (see pages 32 and 35). Other prefixes can be used to add meaning to a base word or word root. Some of these prefixes can be used in more than one way, depending on their context. The exercises on the next two pages look at some of these.

Exercise 1
Match the prefixes on the left with their meaning(s) on the right. Two of these prefixes have one meaning (although used in different ways).

Prefix

1. auto-
2. bi-
3. circum-
4. co-
5. inter-
6. micro-
7. mono-
8. post-
9. pre-
10. semi-
11. sub-
12. tele
13. trans-
14. uni-

Meaning

(a) After or later than.
(b) Between.
(c) Exactly half / partly but not completely.
(d) Across / changing / between.
(e) Together / sharing.
(f) Single / one.
(g) Before.
(h) One small part of a larger thing / below another thing / smaller or less important than another thing.
(i) Two / twice / double.
(j) Around.
(k) Of or by yourself / working by itself.
(l) Extremely small.
(m) At or over a long distance.

Exercise 2
Use the prefixes from the left-hand column above, and the base words / roots from the box below, to form words that can complete definitions 1 – 28. One definition can be completed with two words (using the same prefix).

...annual	...biography	...conference	...determined	...ennial	...ference	...final	...form
...graduate	...habit	...hesion	...ient	...late	...lingual	...mature	...mission	...mutes
...que	...nomy	...ordinate	...organism	...poly	...pone	...precious	...scope	...standard
		...tonous	...val	...vent			

1. A / an _____ student is a student who is studying after receiving an advanced degree such as an M.A. or Ph.D.

2. A / an _____ voice or sound is boring and unpleasant because it does not change its loudness or become higher or lower.

3. Something that is _____ is the same everywhere you find it.

4. When you _____ something, you change spoken or written words into another language.

5. A / an _____ is one of two games, such as football, that are played immediately before the last game in a sports competition.

6. A / an _____ is a short break in the middle of a play, film, concert, etc.

7. _____ is a situation in which people or things combine well to form a unit.

8.   A _____ is a meeting held among people who are in different places, using an electronic communication system such as a computer.

9.   An event that is _____ happens twice every year.

10. An event that is _____ happens once every two years.

11. A / an _____ is the distance measured around the edge of a circle, or the edge of a circle or a round object / area.

12. A / an _____ is a book about your life that you write yourself.

13. If you _____ something, you decide that it will not be done at the time it was planned, but at a later time.

14. If someone finds a way of avoiding a rule or law that limits them, especially by using a clever trick that does not break the law, we can say that they _____ it.

15. A / an _____ is a piece of equipment for looking at things that are too small to see normally.

16. Something that is _____ is very special, unusual, or good, or is not the same as anything or anyone else.

17. If something happens too soon or before its usual time, we can say that it is _____.

18. Something that is _____ is not as good as you would normally expect, or not good enough to be accepted.

19. If two people live together in a physical relationship but are not married, we say that they _____.

20. A / an _____ is a living thing that is so small you cannot see without special equipment (such as that in 15 above).

21. If something _____, it changes into something completely different.

22. A company that has complete control of the product or service it provides because it is the only company that provides it can be said to be, or have, a / an _____.

23. If something is _____, it happens or develops in a particular way because of things that have existed, happened, or been decided before.

24. Someone who is _____ is able to speak two languages very well.

25. If a country, state, region, organization, etc., has _____, it is independent and has the power to govern itself.

26. Something that is _____ exists, happens or stays somewhere for a short period of time only.

27. If a person is _____, he or she has less power or authority than someone else.

28. A / an _____ stone is one that is used in jewelry and is fairly valuable, but not as valuable as other stones such as diamonds or rubies.

Presenting an argument

Exercise 1
Read the text below, in which somebody is trying to decide whether to go straight to university from school, or spend a year traveling around the world. Put their argument into the correct order, using the key words and expressions in **bold** to help you. The first one and last one have been done for you.

A. **(1)** I'm really in two minds about what to do when I leave school. Should I go straight to university or should I spend a year traveling around the world?

B. **It is often said** that knowledge is the key to power, and I cannot disagree with this.

C. **On the one hand**, I would experience lots of different cultures.

D. Unfortunately, **another point is that** if I spent a year traveling I would need a lot of money.

E. And I'm not alone in this opinion. **Many consider** a sound career and a good salary to be an important goal.

F. **However**, it could be argued that I would also meet lots of interesting people while I was traveling.

G. **Secondly**, if I go straight to university, I'll learn so many things that will help me in my future life.

H. **First of all**, there are so many benefits to going straight to university.

I. But **I believe that** it would be easy to make a bit while I was traveling, giving English lessons or working in hotels and stores.

J. **Moreover**, I'll be able to take part in the social activities that the university offers, and meet lots of new friends who share the same interests.

K. **The most important point is that** the sooner I get my qualifications, the quicker I'll get a job and start earning.

L. **Nevertheless**, these inconveniences would be an inevitable part of traveling and would be greatly outweighed by the other advantages.

M. **In my opinion**, starting work and making money is one of the most important things in life.

N. **On the other hand**, I could end up suffering from culture shock, homesickness, and some strange tropical diseases.

O. **Furthermore**, if I spent a year traveling, I would learn more about the world.

P. **(16)** All right, I've made my mind up. Now, where's my nearest travel agency?

Exercise 2.
Using the key words and expressions in **bold** from the last exercise, present an argument for <u>one</u> of the following issues, or choose one of the essays from the Topics section of the book:

1. A government's main priority is to provide education for its people.

2. The only way to save the environment is for governments to impose strict quotas on the energy we use (for example, by restricting car ownership, limiting the water we use).

3. Satisfaction in your job is more important than the money you earn.

4. Living in a town or city is better than living in the countryside.

Pronouns and determiners

<u>Exercise 1</u>

Complete these sentences with an appropriate pronoun or determiner (e.g., his, which, there, itself, etc.). You will need to use some pronouns / determiners more than once.

1.   The team arrived in Cairo, and from _____ set out across the desert in a southwesterly direction.

2.   Students are allowed to hand in _____ assignments a few days late if they ask for permission at least a week in advance.

3.   The new laws made _____ easier to get a passport and travel abroad.

4.   Someone called for you, but you weren't here, so I told _____ you would call when you got back.

5.   Many playwrights like to act in the plays they have written. Shakespeare _____ appeared in productions of his own works.

6.   Most students spend more time on their assignments than _____ should.

7.   Why did you say that I've missed lots of lessons this semester? Where did you get _____ idea? I haven't missed a single one.

8.   Greek and Latin are languages from _____ many English words have been taken or adapted.

9.   Someone broke the printer, but _____ looks like nobody is prepared to accept responsibility.

10.   The company carried out research into chemical fertilizers and _____ effect on the environment.

11.   The drug works in small quantities, but _____ efficacy is reduced if used too much and too often.

12.   _____ comes a time in everyone's life when a big decision has to be taken.

13.   Nuclear energy is far less damaging to the environment than _____ produced from fossil fuels, but requires far higher standards of safety to be applied.

14.   The authors admitted using material from other books, but we had to give _____ credit for their ability to make an otherwise boring subject lively and interesting.

15.   A skilled workforce is essential, _____ is why regular training programs are so important.

16.   The young chick relies on the adult bird for food, and it will be several weeks before it can feed _____.

17.   The vehicle employs a small solar panel, from which _____ can get enough power to move without the need for turning the engine on.

18.   We should give everyone a chance to say what _____ think.

19.   Research in the 1960's often took a lot of time and patience, as there was no Internet in _____ days.

20.   The house stood by _____ on a small island, cut off from the outside world by a treacherous reef.

Exercise 2
Instructions as above.

1.   Her latest book is one _____ every teenager will enjoy.

2.   Help was offered in the first instance to families _____ homes had been destroyed in the tsunami.

3.   The company was forced to cut prices and lay off staff, but the problems didn't end _____.

4.   As it became obvious an economic crisis was looming, the Republicans were divided among _____ as to the best course of action to take.

5.   Bogart's most famous movie was probably Casablanca, _____ was made in 1942.

6.   Prices in New York are roughly 30% cheaper than _____ in London.

7.   People who adopt children tend to be people who have no children of _____ own but who desperately want some.

8.   The voice at the end of the phone was _____ of a young man.

9.   We have tea or coffee: _____ would you prefer?

10.   Most people passed the exam, and _____ that failed were allowed to retake it a month later.

11.   Immigrants often come to the country on their own, and then ask their families to join _____ at a later date.

12.   Those who want to see Las Vegas and sample all of _____ attractions are going to need a lot of money.

13.   AZB Ltd claimed that the invention was legally _____, and sued their competitor for breaching their design copyright.

14.   The Republican Party have come under a lot of pressure, but _____ refuse to bow down to popular pressure.

15.   The winner was a Chinese composer, _____ composition "Blue String" combined elements of classical Chinese and Western music.

16.   We've been thinking about the offer _____ you made last week.

17.   We need to prepare _____ for the struggle that we are about to face.

18.   The software has a few glitches, but the real problem lies in the computer, and not in the software _____.

19.   Fees must be paid in full before the course begins. Alternatively, you can pay _____ in 6 monthly installments through the first semester.

20.   As part of the survey, we asked members of the public questions about _____ their work, their hobbies, how they spent their vacation, and so on.

Also see *Working words* on pages 80 – 81

Similar meanings: Adjectives 1

Here is a crossword with a difference. The words, which are all adjectives, are already in the grid, but some of the letters have been removed. With the help of a dictionary, try to fill in the missing letters. The more letters you fill in, the easier it becomes to complete the grid.

When you have done this, match the adjectives in the grid with a word or expression with a similar meaning which you will find in **bold** on the next page:

1. A **rude** reply.

2. A **strong and successful** economy.

3. **Basic** facilities.

4. A **small** charge for services.

5. **Traditional** medicine.

6. An **inquisitive** student.

7. **Specialist** knowledge.

8. An **isolated** village.

9. A **ridiculous** idea.

10. **Suitable** computer software.

11. A **valid** reason for doing something.

12. **Strict** economic controls.

13. A **calm, peaceful** sea.

14. A **small** margin of opportunity.

15. A **secret** operation.

16. An **insignificant** amount of money

17. **Dangerous** chemicals.

18. An exhibition of **modern** art.

19. **Lasting** appeal.

20. **Extremely unusual** circumstances.

21. **Very strange or unusual** behavior.

22. A **punctual** start to a meeting.

23. **Old-fashioned** ideas.

24. A **potential or likely** candidate for a job.

25. A **thorough** investigation.

26. **Enough** information.

27. **Gradual** progress.

28. A **sudden, sharp** rise in prices.

29. A **flourishing** community.

30. **Difficult and detailed** instructions.

31. A **creative** director.

32. A **powerful** drug.

33. **Extreme** measures to prevent or achieve something.

34. A **superficial** person.

35. **Unpredictable** behavior.

36. **Rich** agricultural soil.

37. A **level** surface.

38. **Very important** information (2 possible words).

39. A **diverse** program of events.   .

40. **Essential** raw materials (2 possible words).

41. **Poisonous** gases.

42. **Clear and direct** comments.

43. **Limited** natural resources.

44. **Extensive** unemployment.

45. A **determined** student.

46. **Rough** material.

Similar meanings: Adjectives 2

Look at sentences 1 – 14 and choose a word from the box that has a similar meaning to the words and expressions in **bold**. Write these words in the grid below. The first one has been done as an example.

If you do it correctly, you will reveal a word in the shaded vertical strip that is a synonym of the word *"typical"* in this sentence:

*The strong sense of community is **typical** of an area where people feel they are an underclass who must struggle to survive.*

| abundant archaic chaotic concise credible evident hypothetical |
| industrious integral rampant risky scrupulous tedious tenacious |

1. His instructions were very **brief and clear**.

2. Here's an **imaginary** situation: you are in the desert and you run out of water.

3. Latin is considered by many to be an **outdated** language, despite the fact that many words from the language are still in use today.

4. From a financial point of view it was a very **dangerous** plan.

5. There are **plenty of** opportunities for promotion if you are prepared to work hard.

6. The conference was really **disorganized** and a complete waste of time.

7. His lectures are **boring** and I never seem to learn anything useful or interesting.

8. It was **obvious** that the President had been told what to say by his advisers.

9. **Uncontrolled** corruption and abuse of power by officials eventually prompted new anti-corruption laws.

10. The setting of the scene in chapter one of the book is **essential** to the plot.

11. He gained a reputation as an **honest and fair** dealer, and therefore won the respect of his customers.

12. He was a **determined** man who believed in fighting for his principles at any cost.

13. She was a serious, **hardworking** student who achieved excellent grades.

14. The story seemed **believable** at first, but a bit of research revealed some startling irregularities.

	First letter	Rest of word
1	c	*oncise*
2		
3		
4		
5		
6		
7		
8		
9		
10		
11		
12		
13		
14		

Similar meanings: Nouns

Exercise 1

Look at sentences 1 – 20. These can either be completed with a word from box A *or* a word with a similar meaning from box B. Identify both the words that could be used. In some cases, you will need to add an -s to one or both of the words when you put them into the sentence.

A	B
acclaim accommodations agenda appeal appointment assistance benefit discipline discount drop fallacy fault means opposition poll proof proximity requirement victory work	advantage closeness decline defect employment evidence help housing meeting method misconception order petition praise prerequisite resistance reduction schedule survey triumph

1.   We have a very busy _____ / _____ today, so I suggest we start as soon as possible.

2.   The college provides cheap _____ / _____ for its staff and students.

3.   With regard to attendance and punctuality, we need to maintain _____ / _____ at all times.

4.   Thank you for your kind _____ / _____: I couldn't have done it without you.

5.   There has been a sharp _____ / _____ in the number of people attending afternoon classes.

6.   The early computer program had several _____ / _____ which need to be sorted out before it could be used.

7.   There has been a lot of _____ / _____ to the new schedule: nobody likes the earlier starts and later finishes to the day.

8.   There is no _____ / _____ to show that standards of living have improved.

9.   Students holding a valid student card are eligible for a 10% _____ / _____ on book prices.

10.   The bar is popular with our students because of its _____ / _____ to the college.

11.   I can't see you this afternoon because I have a / an _____ / _____ with my tutor.

12.   The Turkish writer Orhan Pamuk received international _____ / _____ for his novel "Snow".

13.   At the height of its success, the studio provided _____ / _____ for over 3,000 people.

14.   There are several _____ / _____ to working from home: you save on travel costs, for one thing.

15.   If you want to do a Degree in Middle East Studies, a basic knowledge of Arabic is one of the main _____ / _____

16.   The cheapest _____ / _____ of traveling around the U.S.A. is by Greyhound bus.

17.   The _____ / _____ taken before the election did not reflect the final result.

18.   His ruling in the case was a _____ / _____ for common sense and freedom of speech.

19.   Many people believe that exercising makes you more hungry: this is in fact a _____ / _____.

20.   The _____ / _____ was rejected by the arbitrating committee, despite the fact it had been signed by over 5,000 people.

General Vocabulary

Exercise 2
Instructions as above.

A	B
admission alteration characteristic choice code component cooperation discussion liability magnitude overview priority problem protest question result strategy valid winner zenith	access change collaboration complication consequence deliberation demonstration (short) description element feature good importance option peak plan precedence query responsibility rule victor

1.	The _____ / _____ against the war spread to most parts of the city by midnight, with at least 50 arrests taking place.

2.	The college _____ / _____ state(s) that students must attend at least 80% of their classes.

3.	The college accepts no _____ / _____ for any damage to vehicles in the car park.

4.	There are two _____ / _____ available to you: work hard on improving your mid-term grades, or consider changing your course.

5.	Our latest prospectus provides a / an _____ / _____ of our courses and a brief history of the university.

6.	Nobody understood the _____ / _____ of the results: it was assumed that everything would stay the same, whereas there were in fact profound changes

7.	Thanks to their _____ / _____ with several affiliated companies, they managed to create a virtual monopoly for their product.

8.	I hope you have a _____ / _____ reason for missing so many of your classes.

9.	The empire reached its _____ / _____ at the end of the nineteenth century.

10.	If you have any _____ / _____ please ask a member of staff.

11.	A purple rash and a persistent cough is one of the _____ / _____ of this disease.

12.	We had hoped that everything would run smoothly, but unfortunately there have been several _____ / _____.

13.	Before you start studying for the TOEFL, you should come up with a _____ / _____ that will help you to make the most of your study time.

14.	Safety in the workplace is very important, and should take _____ / _____ over everything else.

15.	Is it necessary to make any _____ / _____ to the plan, or should we keep it as it is?

16.	In the battle of the sexes there can never be a true _____ / _____.

17.	Fieldwork is a key _____ / _____ of this course.

18.	After much _____ / _____, we decided to reject her offer.

19.	Climate change could have disastrous _____ / _____ for farmers.

20.	_____ / _____ to the building after 6 p.m. is limited to staff and full-time students only.

52

Exercise 3
Instructions as above

A	B
achievement advent amenity argument backing category charisma disparity display ending implication invention notion number part proceeds reflection review specialist ultimatum	accomplishment (personal) appeal appearance classification component concentration difference dispute exhibit expert facility final demand earnings idea innovation sign suggestion support termination write-up

1.	The book received a lot of good _____ / _____ in the press, and went on to become one of the year's bestsellers.

2.	Before the _____ / _____ of the home PC in the mid-80s, not many people knew how to type.

3.	Unlike his much-loved father, the young leader lacked _____ / _____ and failed to become popular with his people.

4.	The best English dictionaries are those for English-language learners: dictionaries in this _____ / _____ tend to give very clear definitions with good examples.

5.	The board ordered the _____ / _____ of all research, with the result that it was another five years before a cure for the illness was found.

6.	Technological _____ / _____ have changed the world in the last 20 years.

7.	Large _____ / _____ of unskilled, unemployed people in certain parts of the country have resulted in a rise in crime and street violence.

8.	I'm not an economics _____ / _____, but even I know that a drop in unemployment often leads to a rise in inflation.

9.	With _____ / _____ from her teachers, she was able to start an international languages club at the school.

10.	Our new Economics tutor has a strange _____ / _____ that all students are lazy and irresponsible.

11.	You will find the problem easier to solve if you try breaking it down into its separate _____ / _____.

12.	His promotion to director was a remarkable _____ / _____ for someone so young.

13.	Our head of department gave us a / an _____ / _____ get down to some serious work or get out.

14.	Despite several changes to the pay structure, there is still a _____ / _____ in pay between graduate trainees and non-graduates.

15.	All _____ / _____ from the sale of part of the grounds will be re-invested in the college.

16.	His irrational behavior eventually led to a serious _____ / _____ with his sponsors.

17.	College _____ / _____ include a gym, a swimming pool, a canteen, and a garden where students can relax.

18.	The museum's _____ / _____ of prehistoric tools and artifacts is surprisingly popular with children.

19.	I'm not happy with your _____ / _____ that my work is below standard.

20.	A person's choice of clothes is a / an _____ / _____ of his or her personality.

Similar meanings: Verbs 1

Words with similar meanings are tested in the TOEFL Reading Comprehension. It is also useful to know alternatives to other words to make your writing more varied, and to improve your general reading skills.

Look at the words and expressions in **bold** in the following sentences, and choose a word from the box that has the same or a similar meaning in the same context. Use these words to complete the crossword on page 56. You do not need to change any of the word forms.

accuse	affect	answer	assert	assist	assume	attain	baffle	change	convey	create
demand	derive	detect	direct	elicit	endure	enrich	exceed	evolve	forbid	gather
handle	hasten	launch	mirror	misuse	oblige	obtain	permit	refine	refuse	relate

remove   resist   reveal   settle   submit   verify

Across (◊)

2.   His job is mainly to **control** the activities of everyone in the company with a view to making optimum use of the workforce.

4.   We normally **suppose** that most people nowadays have a computer at home.

5.   Shakespeare said that some people **achieve** greatness, while others have it thrust upon them.

6.   Did you **notice** a hint of pessimism in her report?

11.   He was asked to **disclose** government secrets in exchange for money.

12.   If you want people to take you seriously, you should **state firmly** your reasons for change.

13.   Antibodies help our bodies to **fight** infection.

14.   Several attempts were made to **improve** the system.

15.   Computer software will continue to **develop** in response to users' needs.

16.   They asked us to **give** our thanks and best wishes to the chairman.

19.   The U.S.A. and Iran have often tried to **resolve** their differences, but with little effect.

21.   It took him some time to **tell** the story, and it was late when he eventually finished.

23.   The department was asked to **propose** some ideas for increasing student enrollment.

25.   A revolutionary new scientific method may soon help to **alter** people's physical appearance without the need for surgery.

27.   His explanation seemed to **confuse** most people.

29.   Would you **reply to** his question as briefly as possible.

32.   The device is able to **confirm** whether a banknote is genuine or a forgery by analyzing the paper and print quality.

33. Some plants, such as beans, **benefit** the soil in which they are planted.

35. The rules are designed to **eliminate** obstacles that may discourage investors.

36. Everyone hoped that the results of his research would **surpass** their expectations.

37. Not all foodstuffs that **come** from animals are tested to ensure they are fit for human consumption.

Down (⇔)

1. Crime is a complex issue: we cannot simply **blame** poverty and unemployment.

3. He was asked to **deal with** the situation with tact and discretion.

7. To **make** a new folder, click on the new folder icon at the top of your computer.

8. We were unable to **obtain** the information we needed from the committee.

9. There was general approval when the announcement to **ban** smoking on college premises was made.

10. His inability to act quickly enough will probably **accelerate** their decision to dismiss him.

12. Even a small change in economic circumstances can **influence** our spending habits.

14. Alternative therapies are often suggested for patients who **reject** conventional medical treatment.

17. The report was based on information that they managed to **collect** from all parts of the country.

18. The college rules **require** students to refrain from smoking and drinking inside the faculty buildings.

20. Trends come and go, but there are a few that will always **stay**.

22. To ask for a loan, you will need to **acquire** a form from the student welfare office.

24. It is often argued that not enough laws exist to punish those who **abuse** the Internet.

26. The new technique will **facilitate** rapid identification of possible threats from unstable areas.

28. The company announced it will **introduce** a new version of its software in January.

30. The senator's relaxed attitude to the problem didn't **reflect** those of his constituents.

31. The governor was asked to **insist on** new measures to combat crime.

34. We do not **allow** the use of cellphones in the building.

Similar meanings: Verbs 2

Exercise 1

Rearrange the letters in **bold** at the end of sentences 1 – 16 to make words with the same or a similar meaning to the underlined words and expressions in the sentence. Write your answers in the spaces on the right. The shaded letter in each space is the same as the letter in the **bold** square in the next line. The first one has been done for you.

1. The machine was designed to grind rocks for industrial purposes. **srhcu**

c	r	u	s	h

2. The television campaign helped to increase public awareness of the drug problem. **iehthnge**

3. During the election, the Republicans made a great effort to woo younger voters. **tactart**

4. Many retail outlets are substituting cashiers with automatic machines. **nelarcpig**

5. The new building symbolizes modern American architecture at its best. **pefeliixems**

6. Everyone endorsed the treaty as it was critically important to the peace process. **redpupost**

7. If you want to reclaim the money you have lost, you will have to fill in a claims form. **evroerc**

8. He was asked to account for the changes he had made to the curriculum. **pinelax**

9. More must be done to find other sources of fuel for when we deplete our supply of oil. **hatesxu**

10. It can take a lot of time and effort to acquire the grade you want in the TOEFL. **hiveace**

11. Violence may have been averted if the police had not acted so aggressively. **vredntepe**

12. The media liked to depict the leader as a national hero, when in fact he was a cruel tyrant. **rpryato**

13. We know that there are benefits, but they are very difficult to quantify. **sumreea**

14. The aim of the organization is to promote travel among young people. **oragnceue**

15. The two reports emphasize the problems that are faced by those living in housing projects. **gighihlth**

16. The transformation is accelerated by adding salt to the solution. **satheden**

Exercise 2
Instructions as above.

1. The study <u>confirmed</u> the findings of earlier research.
   vopdre

p	r	o	v	e	d

2. No one was able to <u>unravel</u> the complex mystery surrounding her sudden disappearance.   **vleos**

   (boxes with **v** in fourth box)

3. Travel can <u>broaden</u> your knowledge of the world around you.   **senciare**

4. We wanted to <u>involve</u> the community in our plans for a new sports center.   **ludecin**

5. Their choice was <u>influenced and controlled</u> by political circumstances.   **tatdidce**

6. If you fail to attend classes, you might <u>lose</u> your right to continue studying at the college.   **oeirftf**

7. The exhibition was originally <u>conceived</u> as a tribute to the Bauhaus movement.   **tcedare**

8. The drug was designed to <u>regulate</u> the flow of blood to the brain.   **tcoonlr**

9. The government is committed to <u>promoting</u> the use of public transport.   **gagcuenrino**

10. Wind, tides, and the sun can all be used to <u>generate</u> power.
    douprec

11. We began to <u>think</u> that the project might involve more work than we had planned.   **cpustse**

12. Thousands of young men volunteered to <u>defend</u> their country.   **totprec**

13. Planning regulations <u>limited</u> development on the land outside large towns and cities.   **acostrnidne**

14. They <u>tolerated</u> poor working conditions in order to finish the job quickly.   **petacdec**

15. Before they began, they needed to <u>ascertain</u> that the project was feasible.   **cehkc**

16. Some materials may <u>display</u> the characteristics of both a liquid and a solid.   **itehxib**

Exercise 3
Instructions as above.

1. We quickly <u>perceived</u> the truth about their intentions regarding the environment. **lredzaie**

`r e a l i z e d`

2. Under his reign peace and mutual understanding <u>flourished</u>. **popederrs**

`_ r _ _ _ _ _ _`

3. The results <u>exceeded</u> everyone's expectations. **spsuareds**

4. Political apathy could be <u>interpreted</u> as a sign of satisfaction with the government. **dusneotodr**

5. The new drug considerably <u>enhanced</u> the patients' quality of life. **vimodpre**

6. Governments have been slow to <u>deal with</u> the problems of global warming. **srsaded**

7. They are trying to gather all the facts <u>pertaining</u> to the problem. **tirelagn**

8. The concept of factory outlet shopping <u>began</u> in the U.S.A. **giniaoredt**

9. The foundation was formed specifically to <u>administer</u> the project. **gaamen**

10. Scientists <u>analyzed</u> samples of leaves taken from the area. **meaienxd**

11. Many people are reluctant to <u>eliminate</u> certain food products from their diet. **ervmeo**

12. We all <u>assumed</u> that he would leave when the project was finished. **pedospus**

13. The research failed to <u>yield</u> the information they were looking for. **ocpredu**

14. We didn't <u>accomplish</u> much this week. **vehiace**

15. The crisis was <u>resolved</u> through a series of open talks and compromise. **tlsedte**

16. The company pioneered the idea of selling furniture that customers had to <u>assemble</u> themselves. **diubl**

Spelling

Exercise 1

There are eleven words in this passage which are spelled incorrectly. Can you find and correct them?

Apart from condemming tobacco companies and rising the price of cigarettes, the goverment's anti-smoking campain has failed to have any long-term affects, and the only people bennefitting from it are the Treasury Departement. Meanwhile, some doctors have said that they may refuse to treat persistant smokers. Of course, this hasn't prevented the big tobbaco companys spending vast amounts of money on advertiseing.

Exercise 2

Instructions as above.

It is argueable whether good pronounciation is more important than good grammer and vocabulery. Consientious students balance their aquisition of these skills, hopeing to acheive both fluency and accuracey. Teachers should encourage there students to practice all the relavant language skills.

Exercise 3

Instructions as above.

It is becomming increasingly difficcult for many people to find decent accomodations in Los Angeles at a price they can afford. To put it simpley, most people just don't have the necesary funds. Organizeations such as Home Front can offer advise, but it is widely agreed that the situation is no longer managable. The fact that the LA city council is building cheap, tempory housing for lower-paid profesionals is the only official acknowlegment of this problem.

Exercise 4

Here are some more words which students of English (and many native English speakers) often spell incorrectly. Can you identify and correct the mistake in each case? Be careful: 3 of the words are spelled correctly!

1. reversable	2. proffessional	3. critisize	4. neccesary
5. begining	6. percieve	7. indespensable	8. refering
9. liason	10. tendancy	11. definately	12. embarass
13. address	14. recommend	15. responsable	16. seperate
17. questionaire	18. miniscule	19. intergrate	20. categories
21. wierd	22. iresistible	23. acheivement	24. millenium
25. occurence	26. independant	27. supercede	28. harrassment

Starting and stopping

The box below contains 37 words and phrasal verbs related to *starting* or *stopping* something. You will find these by reading horizontally left to right (↻) and vertically down (↬) only. Try to find as many of these as possible, then use them to complete sentences 1 – 25. In many cases, these sentences can be completed with more than one of the words / expressions. In the case of the verbs, you will need to change the form of some of them (for example, by adding *-ed* to the end).

Note that in the case of phrasal verbs, the verb and the particle can be found directly next to each other (for example, *take off* will appear in the box as *TAKEOFF*).

D	A	B	O	L	I	S	H	A	S	E	T	O	F	F	B	C	D	E	F	G	D
I	I	N	C	E	P	T	I	O	N	C	L	O	S	U	R	E	H	I	J	K	E
S	L	T	O	D	M	T	U	R	N	D	O	W	N	N	Q	U	A	S	H	O	T
S	P	A	U	I	Q	R	E	S	T	I	D	I	S	M	I	S	S	U	V	P	E
U	T	K	T	S	W	K	S	X	Y	N	Z	S	U	S	P	E	N	D	A	U	R
A	A	E	B	C	A	I	T	C	D	I	E	S	H	U	T	D	O	W	N	L	C
D	K	O	R	O	T	C	A	S	B	T	R	E	F	E	M	B	A	R	K	L	E
E	E	F	E	N	E	K	B	U	A	I	A	G	H	I	J	F	R	K	L	O	A
P	U	F	A	T	R	O	L	P	C	A	D	D	M	R	N	I	I	O	P	U	S
H	P	C	K	I	M	F	I	P	K	T	I	E	F	E	S	R	S	Q	R	T	E
A	S	A	U	N	I	F	S	R	O	E	C	L	R	T	E	E	E	Q	V	W	X
S	Y	N	Z	U	N	Y	H	E	U	O	A	E	E	I	T	L	A	U	N	C	H
E	U	C	A	E	A	R	E	S	T	A	T	T	E	R	U	B	I	I	T	O	F
I	A	E	T	O	T	S	S	S	E	R	E	E	Z	E	P	A	N	T	D	Y	O
N	U	L	W	I	E	F	R	E	S	I	G	N	E	P	H	A	S	E	O	U	T
M	E	X	P	E	L	W	R	E	N	B	P	R	E	V	E	N	T	V	C	X	Z

1.   Unfortunately, this afternoon's seminar on the Middle East has been _____ because the speaker is sick.

2.   I can't find the document anywhere on my computer. I must have accidentally _____ it.

3.   The laboratory was forced to end its research project when the sponsoring company _____ and refused to give it any more money.

4.   Because of an _____ of food poisoning recently, the school cafeteria will be closed until further notice.

5.   The company was _____ in 2002, but had to _____ less than a year later.

6.   Before _____ on a long journey, it is very important to make sure you have everything you need.

7.   Several of the airline's crews told the press that they were concerned about the safety of its aircraft, but the airline's owner managed to _____ the story before it went public.

8. As a result of increased security and a bigger police presence, crime has been almost completely _____.

9. The library installed security cameras to _____ students from stealing books, but without much success.

10. We tried to _____ the manager from making changes to the company structure, but he said he had already _____ the first stage of the plan.

11. When the product was first _____ onto the market in 1981, there was little public interest. However, after a concerted marketing campaign, sales rapidly _____.

12. Owing to technical problems, use of the college IT center has been temporarily _____ while the computers are checked for viruses.

13. I _____ photography as a hobby when I was 13, but by the time I was 15 I had already decided to make it my career.

14. The new regulations will not all begin at once: they will be gradually _____ over the next two years. Meanwhile, the old system will be gradually _____.

15. Between its _____ in 1925 and its eventual _____ in 2002, World Film Studios made over 300 movies.

16. Hostilities between the major powers _____ in November 1918 after an armistice was signed.

17. Professor Vettriano is 64, so I guess he'll be _____ soon. I think he'll miss working here, though.

18. I had had enough working there and was about to tell my boss I was going to _____ when she called me into her office and told me I was _____!

19. They made an excellent offer, but we were obliged to _____ it _____ because we were working on too many other projects.

20. Course fees have risen rapidly over the last three years, but last week the college announced a _____; they have promised no more fee increases until the end of next year.

21. The student book discount program has been _____. From now on, students will have to pay the full price for all their books.

22. When Congress agreed to _____ the old tax laws, smaller companies suddenly found themselves much better off.

23. We have a lot of things to discuss at this meeting, so I suggest we _____ immediately with a report on last year's sales.

24. Several problems have _____ recently as a result of staff illness. One of these is that fact that two courses we had planned are no longer going to go ahead.

25. Five students have been _____ from the college for using drugs.

Task commands

Complete the second sentence in each pair so that it has the same or a similar meaning to the first sentence. In each case, you need one word only. The first and last letters of each word are in their correct place. Use the words to complete the crossword on the next page.

<u>Across (⇕)</u>

2.
- Recognize and understand the problems that low-income groups face in the U.S.A.
- I_____y the problems faced by low-income groups in the U.S.A.

4.
- Explain why violence on the streets of our cities is becoming more common.
- A_____t for the increase in violence on the streets of our cities.

6.
- Give reasons why protecting the countryside around cities is important.
- A_____e the case for protecting the countryside around cities.

8.
- Describe how nuclear technology has developed over a period of time.
- T_____e the development of nuclear technology.

9.
- Say how much it will cost to set up your own website, either by guessing or by using available information to calculate it.
- E_____e the cost of setting up your own website.

12.
- Look at the differences between the way young people live in your country with the way they do in the U.S.A.
- C_____e the lifestyle of young people in your country with those in the U.S.A.

13.
- Explain clearly and exactly what the word "terrorism" means.
- D_____e the word "terrorism".

15.
- Explain, with clear examples, why it is important to eat healthily.
- I_____e the importance of a healthy diet.

16.
- Carefully consider and calculate the ways your English has improved since you started using this book.
- A_____s the improvements you have made in your English since you started using this book.

17.
- Say what you think will happen with space travel and exploration in the future.
- P_____t the future of space travel and exploration.

18.
- Study carefully the things that cause global warming.
- E_____e the causes of global warming.

<u>Down (⇔)</u>

1.
- Say or write down your career plans for the future, but just give the main points, and don't go into detail.
- O_____e your career plans for the future.

3.
- Give more details than you have already given on how mass globalization is affecting developing countries.
- E_____e on the effects of mass globalization in developing countries.

5.
- Provide a short account of the most important aspects of the role the United Nations has had since 1945.
- S_____e the role United Nations has played since 1945.

7.
- Show me how this computer works by using it yourself.
- D_____e how this computer works.

10.
- Think carefully about how useful a new student social center would be before making a judgement.
- E_____e how useful a new student social center would be.

11.
- Study or explain in detail what is happening around the world as a result of climatic change.
- A_____e the effects of climatic change around the world.

13.
- Write or talk in detail about the advantages and disadvantages of growing up in a big city.
- D_____s the advantages and disadvantages of growing up in a big city.

14.
- Give good reasons why the government spends so much on defense.
- J_____y the government's excessive spending on defense.

Exercise 1

Use the time clauses in the boxes to complete the sentences. Pay particular attention to the words that come before or after the time clause.

Part 1: One action or situation occurring before another action or situation

prior to   previously   earlier   formerly   precede   by the time

1.   .... the advent of the Industrial Revolution, pollution was virtually unheard of.

2.   .... the army had restored order, the city had been almost completely devastated.

3.   ....known as Burma, the republic of Myanmar is undergoing a slow and painful political transformation.

4.   A sudden drop in temperature will usually .... a blizzard.

5.   It was my first trip on an airplane.   .... I'd always gone by train.

6.   The President made a speech praising charity organizations working in Mozambique. ....that day he had promised massive economic aid to stricken areas.

Part 2: One action or situation occurring at the same time as another action

while / as / just as   during / throughout   at that very moment   in the meantime / meanwhile

1.   .... the senator was making his speech, thousands of demonstrators took to the streets.

2.   .... the speech they jeered and shouted slogans.

3.   The senator continued speaking.   .... the police were ordered onto the streets.

4.   He finished the speech with a word of praise for the police.   .... the sun came out and shone down on the angry demonstrators.

Part 3: One action or situation occurring after another action or situation

afterward   as soon as / once / the minute that   following

1.   .... the earthquake, emergency organizations around the world swung into action.

2.   .... the stock market collapsed, there was panic buying on an unprecedented scale.

3.   The Klondike gold rush lasted from 1896 to 1910.   .... the area became practically deserted overnight.

Exercise 2

Look at the words and expressions in the box below and on the next page, and decide if we usually use them to talk about (1) the past, (2) the past leading to the present, (3) the present, or (4) the future.

for the next few weeks   as things stand   ever since   in medieval times   one day

nowadays   from now on   back in the 1990s   over the past six weeks

over the coming weeks and months   in another five years' time   in those days

a few decades ago   lately   at this moment in time   at the turn of the century

in my childhood / youth	at this point in history	by the end of this year
for the foreseeable future	for the past few months	last century
these days	from 1996 to 1998	sooner or later

Exercise 3

There are a lot of idioms and other expressions that use the word "time" in English. In this exercise, you should match the first part of each sentence on the left with its second part on the right, using the expressions in **bold** to help you.

1. I'm very busy at the moment, but I'll try to **make**…	(a) … **time warp**.
2. Don is a really nice man. I **have a lot of**…	(b) … **times out of ten** she's punctual.
3. Susanna is so old-fashioned. She seems to be **living in a**…	(c) … **time for everything**, I suppose.
4. I would love a vacation, but I never seem to **find**…	(d) … **the time comes**.
5. We thought we would be late, but we arrived **with**…	(e) … **time**, too.
6. Shall we start now? After all, **there's no**…	(f) … **the time**.
7. At last, here comes our bus. **About**…	(g) … **time being**.
8. Chris is sometimes late, but **nine**…	(h) … **time to time** it can be glorious.
9. We really need to hurry. There's **no**…	(i) … **time will tell**.
10. I don't want to make a decision now; I'll decide **when**…	(j) … **the times**.
11. I don't know if we will be successful; **only**…	(k) … **time now**.
12. I'm not really watching this movie; I'm just **killing**…	(l) … **time around**.
13. If the company is going to compete successfully, we will need to **move with**…	(m) … **his time**.
14. I've never had Japanese food before, but **there's a first**…	(n) … **time to spare**.
15. If we don't win this time, we will the **second**…	(o) … **time for** him.
16. Picasso was a remarkable artist who was years **ahead of**…	(p) … **time** until my friends arrive.
17. Winters here are generally cold and gray, but **from**…	(q) … **the time** to see you later.
18. I'm thinking of changing jobs in the future, but I'll continue working here **for the**…	(r) … **time to lose**.
19. This isn't a sudden decision. I've been thinking of moving **for some**…	(s) … **the time** for one.
20. My students just aren't interested in their lessons. They don't even listen to me **half**…	(t) … **time like the present**.

Word association: Adjectives

Complete each of the following sentences with one adjective. This adjective should be one that is often used (i.e., it *collocates*) with the nouns and / or adverbs in *italics*. To help you, the first and last letters of each word have been given to you, and there is a sample sentence to show you how that adjective could work with one of the nouns or adverbs.

The first one has been done as an example.

1. C_*AREFU*_L is often followed by the nouns *analysis, assessment, consideration, deliberation, examination, observation,* or *planning.*

   (Sample sentence: *After _____ observation, we noticed that the drug was beginning to take effect*).

2. C_____L is often followed by the nouns *argument, aspect, debate, feature, idea, importance, issue, role,* or *theme.*

   (Sample sentence: *The _____ theme of his talk was the possibility of interstellar travel*).

3. C_____L is often followed by the nouns *analysis, appraisal, evaluation, examination,* or *scrutiny.*

   (Sample sentence: *They carried out a _____ examination of the documents to see if they were genuine*).

4. D_____G is often followed by the nouns *consequence, effect, impact, result, admission, allegation, criticism,* or *disclosure.*

   (Sample sentence: *After a series of _____ allegations about his professional misconduct, he resigned*).

5. E_____L is often followed by the nouns *characteristic, component, element, feature, ingredient, part,* or *requirement.*

   (Sample sentence: *A working knowledge of Spanish is an _____ requirement if you want the job*).

6. F_____E is often followed by the nouns *accusation, allegation, assumption, belief, claim, description, impression,* or *statement.* It is often preceded by the adverbs *blatantly, completely, entirely, patently, totally,* or *utterly.*

   (Sample sentence: *She made several _____ assumptions about her new professor*).

7. I_____T is often followed by the nouns *aspect, element, factor, feature, issue, part,* or *point.* It is often preceded by the adverbs *crucially, extremely, particularly, terribly,* or *vitally.*

   (Sample sentence: *It is vitally _____ to disconnect the appliance from the power supply before dismantling it*).

8. I_____E is often preceded by the adverbs *absolutely, almost, nearly, practically, quite, seemingly, totally, utterly,* or *virtually.*

   (Sample sentence: *I found the language practically _____ to learn*).

9. I_____D is often preceded by the adverbs *deeply, extremely, genuinely, keenly, mainly, particularly, primarily, principally,* or *seriously.*

   (Sample sentence: *I like 19th century art, but I'm primarily _____ in the pre-Raphaelite movement*).

10. L_____Y is often followed by the nouns *delay, discussion, interview, negotiations, pause,* or *period.*

    (Sample sentence: *After a _____ pause, she continued speaking*).

11. M_____R is often followed by the nouns *breakthrough, pause, change, concern, contribution, drawback, factor, influence, obstacle, problem, setback, source,* or *upheaval.*

(Sample sentence: *The withdrawal of sponsorship was a _____ setback to our plans*).

12. M_____L is often followed by the nouns *goods, possessions, prosperity, resources, rewards, wealth,* or *well-being.*

(Sample sentence: *He believed in the principles of life, liberty and the pursuit of _____ wealth*).

13. M_____T is often preceded by the adverbs *comparatively, fairly, quite, rather, relatively, suitably, surprisingly,* or *very.*

(Sample sentence: *Everyone said he was arrogant and boastful, but when I interviewed him, I found him to be surprisingly _____ about his achievements*).

14. N_____E is often followed by the nouns *change, difference, drop, improvement,* or *increase.*

(Sample sentence: *There has been a _____ increase in the cost of living over the last three years*).

15. O_____E is often followed by the nouns *analysis, assessment, description, evaluation,* or *measurement.* It is often preceded by the adverbs *completely, entirely, purely, totally, truly,* or *wholly.*

(Sample sentence: *We tried to capture a purely _____ record of what we heard and saw*).

16. P_____R is often followed by the nouns *attention, concern, emphasis, importance, need, relevance,* or *significance.*

(Sample sentence: *When you are writing an essay, you should pay _____ attention to cohesion of ideas*).

17. P_____R is often followed by the nouns *belief, misconception, myth, opinion,* or *view.*

(Sample sentence: *It is a _____ misconception that men are better drivers than women*).

18. P_____E is often followed by the nouns *approach, attitude, feedback, outlook, reinforcement, response,* or *view.*

(Sample sentence: *His presentation was well-received, and he got a lot of _____ feedback*).

19. R_____D is often followed by the nouns *change, decline, deterioration, expansion, growth, increase, progress, rise,* or *succession.*

(Sample sentence: *The computer industry went through several _____ changes when the Internet was introduced to the public for the first time*).

20. R_____L is often followed by the nouns *approach, argument, choice, decision, explanation, hypothesis,* or *thought.*

(Sample sentence: *We need to make a _____ choice that is based on our needs and on our available funds*).

21. R_____C is often followed by the nouns *alternative, assessment, attitude, chance, estimate, expectation, goal, option, prospect, target,* or *view.*

(Sample sentence: *When you are studying for the TOEFL, you should try to set yourself _____ targets, and not try to do too much too quickly*).

22. S_____E is often followed by the nouns *difficulty, hardship, problem, recession, setback, shortage,* or *threat.*

(Sample sentence: *Earlier settlers in the region faced _____ hardship, and many died young from illness and starvation*).

Word association: Nouns

Complete each of the following sentences with one noun. This noun should be one that is often used (i.e., it *collocates*) with the verbs, adjectives, and other words in *italics*. Use these words to fill in the crossword on page 71.

To help you, the first and last letters of each word have been given to you.

<u>Across (♢)</u>

1. B_____d is often preceded by the words *cultural, disadvantaged, educational, ethnic, middle-class, privileged, religious, social,* or *working class.*

5. An action can have a / an *adverse, beneficial, cumulative, damaging, detrimental, dramatic, harmful, immediate, major, negative, positive, profound, serious, significant,* or *substantial* e_____t on something.

7. When they speak, a person might have a *broad, heavy, pronounced, strong, thick,* or *unmistakable* a_____t.

8. If you are not sure about the answer to a question, you can take a / an *educated, good, informed, inspired, lucky, rough,* or *wild* g_____s.

11. You can *accept, ask for, follow, get, give, ignore, obtain, offer, provide, receive, take,* or *want* a_____e to / from someone.

12. You can give a problem *careful, detailed, due,* or *serious* c_____n.

14. A s_____n can be *constructive, helpful, positive, practical, sensible,* or *tentative.* You can *adopt, make, offer, oppose, reject, submit, volunteer,* or *welcome* one of these.

15. You can *disobey, disregard, follow, give, ignore, issue, obey, provide,* or *repeat* an i_____n.

17. A s_____n to a problem or dispute can be *ideal, optimal, peaceful, possible, practical, satisfactory, simple,* or *workable.*

19. You can *ask, deny, gain, get, give, grant, obtain, receive, refuse, request,* or *seek* p_____n to do something.

20. You can *encounter, experience, face, find,* or *have* d_____y with something.

21. A q_____n can be *academic, educational, formal, professional, specialist,* or *vocational.* You can *acquire, gain, get, have, hold, obtain,* or *possess* one of these.

22. O_____y is often preceded by the adjectives *ample, excellent, golden, great, ideal, lost, missed, perfect, rare,* or *unique.* It is also often preceded by the verbs *miss, offer, provide, seize,* or *take.*

25. When you are trying to guess or calculate something, you can make a / an *accurate, conservative, realistic, reliable,* or *rough* e_____e.

29. A product or a person can have *broad, mass, popular, universal,* or *wide* a_____l.

32. You can *collect, destroy, gather,* or *produce* e_____e that something has been done. This can be *admissible, circumstantial, conclusive, incriminating, sufficient,* or *supporting.*

33. M_____e can be *alternative, complementary, conventional, herbal, holistic, orthodox,* or *traditional.*

34. When you do something, you usually have a / an *compelling, good, legitimate, logical, main, major, obvious, simple,* or *valid* r_____n for doing it.

Down (⌄)

2. If you are not careful, or if you are unlucky, you might be involved in a *bad, fatal, horrific, minor, nasty, serious,* or *tragic* a_____t.

3. You can *accept, assume, bear, exercise, fulfill, shoulder,* or *take* r_____y for your (or someone else's) actions.

4. You can *conclude, negotiate, reach, secure,* or *sign* an a_____t.

6. An object can have *distinctive, important, interesting, key, main, special, striking,* or *unusual* f_____s.

9. If someone has a rather "negative" personality, their b_____r can be *aggressive, antisocial, bad, disruptive, insulting, threatening,* or *violent*.

10. You can have a *brilliant, checkered, distinguished, glittering, promising, successful,* or *varied* c_____r.

12. When you work as part of a team, you can make a *great, huge, important, major, outstanding, positive, significant, useful,* or *valuable* c_____n to the team and its activities.

13. You can give a / an *accurate, brief, detailed, full, general, vague,* or *vivid* d_____n of something.

16. C_____m of something (for example, a book or the actions of a politician) can be *adverse, fierce, outspoken, severe, strong,* or *widespread*.

18. You can *conduct, demand, launch, order, require,* or *undertake* an i_____n into something.

23. For actions and achievements, you can *command, deserve, earn, gain, have, lose, show,* or *win* r_____t. This can be *considerable, deep, genuine, healthy, mutual,* or *proper*.

24. When doing something complicated, you can *adopt, apply, choose, develop, devise, employ, pioneer, provide,* or *use* a m_____d that makes it easier or more effective.

26. A s_____e can be *alphabetical, chronological, logical, numerical,* or *random*.

27. J_____t can be *affected, delivered, exercised, formed, given, impaired, made, passed, reserved,* or *suspended*.

28. You can undertake a / an *ambitious, collaborative, individual, innovative, joint, major, minor, special,* or *specific* p_____t.

30. You can *assess, chart, check, evaluate, follow, hamper, hinder, impede, monitor, obstruct, review, slow, track,* or *watch* the p_____s of something.

31. If someone does something wrong, you might teach them a *hard, harsh, important, salutary,* or *valuable* l_____n.

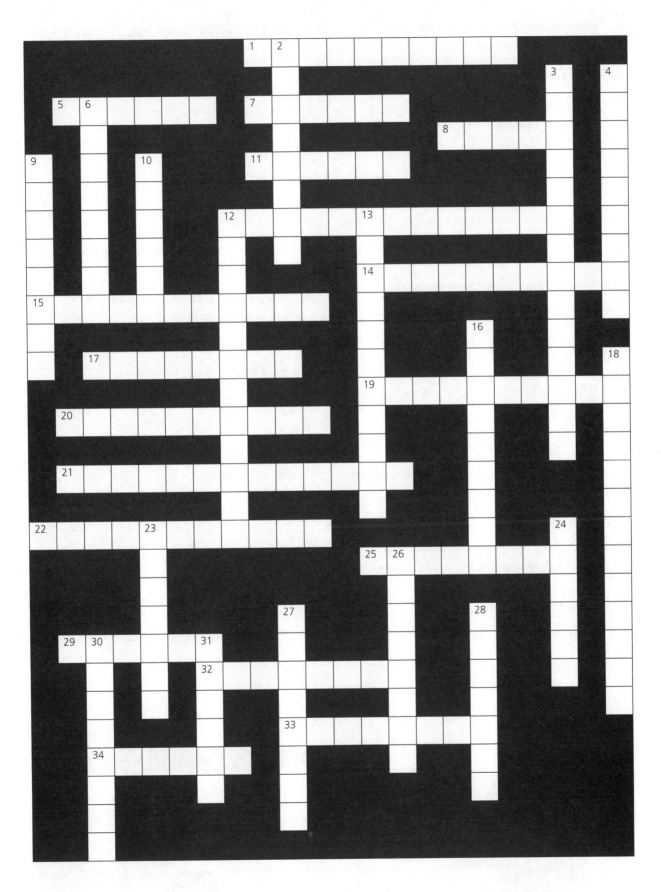

Word association: Verbs

Exercise 1

Complete each of the following sentences with one verb. This verb should be one that is often used (i.e., it *collocates*) with the nouns and / or adverbs in *italics*. To help you, the first and last letters of each word have been given to you, and there is a sample sentence to show you how that verb could work with one of the nouns or adverbs.

Write your answers in the appropriate spaces in the grid. If you do this correctly, you will reveal a word in the shaded vertical strip that is often used with one of these nouns: *authority, confidence, credibility, legitimacy, morale, positions* or *stability* (for example, *"He's very worried about his exams, so we don't want to do anything that might _____ his confidence any further"*).

1.   You can i_____e someone's or something's *behavior, choice, decision, development, outcome, or policy.*

        (Sample sentence: *I don't want to _____ your decision in any way*).

2.   You can o_____n *approval, authorization, consent, evidence, funding, information, license, or permission.*

        (Sample sentence: *You need to _____ permission to use the computers in the library*).

3.   You can d_____s an *issue, a matter, a plan, a proposal, a question, a subject, or a topic.*

        (Sample sentence: *We're all very tired. I suggest we _____ the matter tomorrow*).

4.   You can s_____e *an argument, a conflict, a dispute, a quarrel, or your differences.*

        (Sample sentence: *Neither side showed any willingness to _____ the dispute*).

5.   You can *actively, greatly, positively* or *strongly* e_____e someone or something.

        (Sample sentence: *When I was young, my parents actively _____ me to read as much as possible*).

6.   You can c_____y with a *demand, legislation, an order, a regulation, a request, a requirement, or a rule.*

        (Sample sentence: *You are legally obliged to _____ with the regulations*).

7.   You can d_____e a *mechanism, a method, a plan, a scheme, a strategy, or a system.*

        (Sample sentence: *He _____ a cunning plan to help his friend*).

8.   You can u_____r a *conspiracy, evidence, a fact, a fraud, a mystery, a plot, a scandal, a secret, or the truth.*

        (Sample sentence: *The investigation _____ a scandal that would bring down the government*).

9.   You can d_____e *credit, a mention, praise, recognition, respect, or support.*

        (Sample sentence: *They _____ a lot of praise for all their hard work*).

1.												
2.												
3.												
4.												
5.												
6.												
7.												
8.												
9.												

Exercise 2

Follow the same instructions as Exercise 1. This time, the word you will reveal in the shaded vertical strip is one that is often used with the nouns *agreement, ceasefire, contract, deal, price, settlement, terms, treaty,* or *truce* (for example, *"After the unions refused to end the strike, the management attempted to _____ a new contract"*).

1. You can i_____e *affection, awe, confidence, devotion, envy, loyalty,* or *respect* in other people.

   (Sample sentence: *His actions did little to _____ confidence in his friends and coworkers*).

2. You can o_____t *bitterly, formally, strenuously, strongly, vehemently,* or *vigorously* about something.

   (Sample sentence: *She _____ vehemently when she was accused of cheating*).

3. You can a_____e *consistently, convincingly, forcefully, passionately, persuasively, plausibly,* or *strongly* for or about something.

   (Sample sentence: *They _____ forcefully for a change to the existing rules*).

4. You can o_____e something *bitterly, fiercely, implacably, strenuously, strongly, vehemently,* or *vigorously*.

   (Sample sentence: *Darwin's theories are still bitterly _____ by many people*).

5. You can f_____t *corruption, crime, discrimination, prejudice,* or *terrorism*. You can do this *desperately, doggedly, hard, stubbornly,* or *tenaciously*.

   (Sample sentence: *The new government promised the electorate that it would _____ corruption at all levels*).

6. You can h_____t *a danger, a difference, a difficulty, a fact, the importance (of something), an issue, a need (for something), the plight (of something), a problem,* or *a weakness*.

   (Sample sentence: *Her report _____ the plight of migrant workers in the state*).

7. You can c_____e something or someone *completely, considerably, dramatically, drastically, fundamentally, radically,* or *significantly*.

   (Sample sentence: *Global warming is believed to have radically _____ the climate in some parts of the world*).

8. You can u_____e *an analysis, an assessment, an investigation, a program, a project, research, a review, a study, a survey,* or *a task*.

   (Sample sentence: *The board promised to _____ a review of current working practices*).

9. Something or someone can d_____r *considerably, greatly, markedly, radically, sharply, significantly, substantially,* or *widely* from something or someone else.

   (Sample sentence: *English _____ markedly from Spanish in that the words are not always pronounced as they are written*).

1.												
2.												
3.												
4.												
5.												
6.												
7.												
8.												
9.												

Exercise 3

Follow the same instructions as Exercises 1 and 2. This time, the word you will reveal in the shaded vertical strip is one that is often used with the nouns *attitude*, *belief*, *idea*, *impression*, *notion*, *stereotype*, *tendency*, *trend*, or *view* (for example, "*The latest figures _____ the view that young people read less than they used to*").

1. You can *heartily, thoroughly, warmly, wholeheartedly, officially, overwhelmingly, personally*, or *unanimously* a_____e of someone or something.

   (Sample sentence: *We wholeheartedly _____ the measures that you have taken to boost morale*).

2. You can l_____n to something or someone *attentively, carefully, closely, hard, intently*, or *closely*.

   (Sample sentence: *_____ carefully, because I will say this only once*).

3. You can d_____s an allegation, a claim, an idea, a notion, a suggestion, or a theory.

   (Sample sentence: *She _____ my allegation as a complete fabrication, and more or less accused me of lying*).

4. You can a_____n *a belief, a claim, a commitment, a concept, an idea, a policy*, or *a principle*.

   (Sample sentence: *He used to be quite religious, but _____ his beliefs when his wife died in a road accident*).

5. Something can f_____l *dramatically, rapidly, sharply, slightly, steadily*, or *steeply*.

   (Sample sentence: *Unemployment figures _____ dramatically under the government's "Work or Starve" initiative*).

6. You can c_____t *crime, discrimination, disease, fraud, inflation, poverty, racism, terrorism, unemployment*, or *violence*.

   (Sample sentence: *The organization's main mission statement is to _____ disease and poverty on developing nations*).

7. Someone or something can u_____e *a difficulty, a fact, the importance (of something), the need (for something), a point, a problem*, or *the significance (of something)*.

   (Sample sentence: *The survey results _____ the need for change in people's attitudes toward the homeless*).

8. You can c_____e *an agreement, a contract, a deal, a pact*, or *a treaty*.

   (Sample sentence: *At the end of the summit, an agreement was _____ under which trade sanctions between both countries would be lifted*).

9. You can o_____e *a barrier, a difficulty, a disadvantage, a fear, a hurdle, limitations, an obstacle, a problem, resistance*, or *a weakness*.

   (Sample sentence: *Hypnosis helped him to _____ his fear of flying*).

1.	■								■	
2.							■		■	
3.								■	■	
4.	■								■	
5.	■		■	■	■				■	
6.	■	■	■						■	
7.									■	
8.	■								■	
9.	■									

Word forms: Nouns from verbs

Exercise 1

The verbs in the top box can all be made into nouns by removing and / or adding letters. Decide on the noun form of each verb, and then write it (in its noun form) in the appropriate section of the table, depending on the changes that are made to it. There are five words for each section of the table, and there are 10 words that do not fit into any section of the table.

consume   negotiate   provide   expose   choose   supervise   qualify   admire   persuade   fail   sign   argue   permit   refuse   apply   solve   emphasize   subscribe   disturb   scrutinize   attend   prove   expect   identify   require   coincide   criticize   recognize   warn   survive   acquire   assure   intervene   abolish   arrive   manage   expand   lose   recommend   maintain   determine   rehearse   respond   suggest   prohibit   consult   decide   notify   relax   produce   prefer   imply   behave   compete   promote

Remove 2 letters, then add 4 letters:	(Example: conclude → conclu~~de~~ → conclu<u>sion</u>)
Remove 1 letter, then add 7 letters:	(Example: verify → verif~~y~~ → verif<u>ication</u>)
Remove 1 letter, then add 5 letters:	(Example: examine → examin~~e~~ → examin<u>ation</u>)
Remove 1 letter, then add 4 letters:	(Example: reduce → reduc~~e~~ → reduc<u>tion</u>)
Remove 1 letter, then add 3 letters:	(Example: concentrate → concentrat~~e~~ → concentra<u>tion</u>)
Remove 1 letter, then add 2 letters:	(Example: disperse → dispers~~e~~ → dispers<u>al</u>)

Add 3 letters:	(Example: depart → depart<u>ure</u>)
Add 4 letters:	Example: improve → improve<u>ment</u>)
Add 5 letters:	(Example: confirm → confirm<u>ation</u>)

Exercise 2

Now take the verbs from the box that did *not* fit into any of the sections above, change them into nouns and write them in the grid below (in the same order that they appear in the box). If you do this correctly, you will reveal a word in the shaded vertical strip that can be a verb and a noun *without changing its form*.

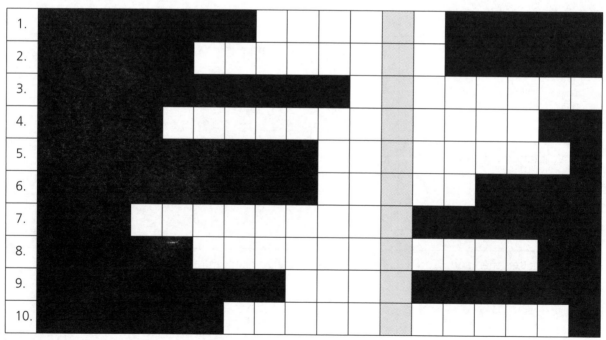

Now try using some of the words from this exercise in sentences of your own.

Word forms: Nouns from adjectives

Exercise 1

Change the adjective in **bold** in each of these sentences to a noun so that the word is grammatically correct in the sentence.

1.   Items of **valuable** can be left in the safe at reception.

2.   Money cannot make up for bad **tasteful** and bad manners.

3.   Do you have a **thirsty** for knowledge? Then why not enroll on one of our evening college courses?

4.   It is often said that "**honest** is the best policy".

5   It can often be lack of **confident** that prevents a student from maximizing his or her potential.

6.   Many people heading off to college for the first time are often unaware of the **expensive** involved in simple day-to-day life.

7.   Student discounts are offered on most products and services on our website, although some **restricted** apply.

8.   There were a few **similar** between the Boeing 727 and the Tupolev 154, but these were mainly cosmetic.

9.   The Director of Studies is unable to say with any **certain** when the new changes will be implemented.

10.   Unnecessary **absent** from work is costing American companies millions of dollars a year.

11.   Please complete the form and return it at your earliest **convenient**.

12.   The student union has questioned the **necessary** of CCTV in the library, but the management insists it is necessary in order to reduce petty theft.

13.   Despite a **relaxed** of regulations, many feel that they are under too much pressure to conform to a set out outdated rules.

14.   Sometimes in business, rules have to be changed according to needs: **flexible** is the key to success.

15.   Health and **safe** issues should be a priority with any organization.

16.   The management accepts no **responsible** for items lost or stolen in the cafeteria and immediate area.

17.   In advertising, **accurate** is very important when it comes to identifying the target market.

18.   The legal **professional** is often criticized for concentrating on making money instead of upholding the law.

19.   There were several unforeseen **complicated** with the new airport extension owing to opposition from environmental groups.

20. Do you know the **different** between net profit and gross profit? Is overtime the same as allowed time? If you answered "no" to the first and "yes" to the second, it's time you joined our "Business for Basics" course!

21. His success and popularity were probably due in part to his wonderful **charismatic**.

22. There is a growing problem of drug **addicted** in our cities.

23. The U.S. **constitutional** guarantees freedom of the press.

24. As soon as the **investigative** is complete, we can make a decision.

25. There can be no **justified** for paying health workers so little money.

26. By the time he was thirty, he was no longer able to differentiate between fantasy and **real**.

Exercise 2

Change the adjectives in the box into nouns following the instructions in the table. Each instruction relates to 3 of the adjectives in the box.

able   aggressive   appreciative   available   aware   bored   comfortable   compatible   confused
considerate   convenient   creative   deep   familiar   fashionable   functional   high   hot   logical
long   loyal   mature   optimistic   optional   pessimistic   popular   punctual   realistic   secure
serious   strong   sufficient   systematic   true   warm   weak

Remove 4 letters:	
Remove 3 letters, then add 5 letters:	
Remove 3 letters, then add 1 letter:	
Remove 2 letters, then add 5 letters:	
Remove 2 letters, then add 3 letters:	
Remove 2 letters, then add 2 letters:	
Remove 2 letters:	
Remove 1 letter, then add 3 letters:	
Remove 1 letter, then add 2 letters:	
Add 2 letters:	
Add 3 letters:	
Add 4 letters:	

Try to use some of the words above in some of your own sentences.

Word forms: Adjectives from verbs

Change the verbs in **bold** into their correct adjective form so that they are grammatically correct in the context of the sentences.

1. At the recruitment drive we were shown a lot of **promote** material, but it wasn't very **inspire**.

2. Recently, there have been some **innovate** and **impress** plans to change the student social areas.

3. In the interests of the environment, we all need to change their **waste** habits, so the college is introducing an **oblige** code for recycling and cutting down on waste.

4. The task we were given was very **repeat** and as a result it quickly became very **bore**.

5. Everybody was very **excite** when we were told about the cultural trip to Europe, but I was a little **doubt** it would go ahead.

6. Our new Director of Studies isn't very **decide** and needs to play a more **act** role in the day-to-day running of the college.

7. Computer software designers need to be far more **invent** if they want to keep up with a changing and **change** market.

8. The Coke and coffee machines have both been out of order five times this week, and the air conditioning hasn't been working for a month: these **continue** breakdowns, coupled with the **continue** heat, have resulted in a lot of short tempers.

9. My tutor isn't very **approach**: in fact, some of my fellow students find him a little bit **frighten**!

10. Her presentation wasn't very **convince**, and several of her classmates were extremely **criticize** of her arguments.

11. The market for all-**include** holidays (in which customers pay for their flight, accommodations, meals, and drinks in advance) has become very **compete**.

12. Our tutor is very **help** and **support**, but unfortunately he isn't very **depend**.

13. The mistake was easily **rectify**, but it would have been far more **prefer** if it hadn't happened in the first place.

14. Fees are non-**negotiate**, and you will need to pay a non-**refund** deposit of $500 before we can enroll you.

15. There is **restrict** access to the building, and all visitors will need to show a **validate** pass and some form of ID.

16. Participation in the evening training seminars is entirely **volunteer**, but we hope that everyone will attend these highly **construct** sessions.

17. The accident was **avoid**, and it wouldn't have happened if you hadn't been so **care**.

18. He's a very **create** and **imagine** artist, and his commitment to helping young painters is **admire**.

19. When you apply for a job, it is very important to be **specify** about your **occupy** qualifications, and any previous experience.

20. A good job should offer an **attract** salary and other **excel** benefits, such as a company car and free healthcare package.

21. The two comments were **contradict**, and it was clear the student who wrote the essay wasn't very **enthuse** about his subject.

22. An **act** lifestyle is **prefer** to a sedentary one, and is certainly much healthier.

Working words

This exercise lets you review some of the more common uses of "grammar"-type words (prepositions, conjunctions, pronouns, prepositions, etc.) in context. Use **one** word to complete each gap in the sentences. In some cases, there may be more than one alternative answer, but you should just give one of them.

1. I'm afraid _____ say you have absolutely _____ chance _____ passing the exam.

2. A few years _____, people _____ to write letters to each other. _____ days, it's all e-mails and text messages.

3. You can't leave early, _____ if you promise to work late tomorrow.

4. _____ 1999 and 2003, the book sold _____ a million copies.

5. One or two of my friends live abroad, but _____ of them live _____ my home.

6. Please _____ quiet. I'm trying to concentrate _____ my project.

7. _____ it rains tomorrow, we can go _____ a picnic.

8. We wanted to see the exhibition _____ the art gallery, but knowing how _____ other people _____ be there, we decided to give it a miss.

9. In _____ of missing most of his lessons, he _____ to pass the exam.

10. I adore spicy food. _____ is the reason I'm so keen _____ Mexican cooking.

11. Jan Kelly, a teacher _____ works at St. Clare's in Portland, Oregon, has _____ been given a "Teacher of the Year" award.

12. He approached his English lessons _____ enthusiasm, and _____ excellent progress as a result.

13. His sudden change of heart took everyone _____ surprise, since previously he _____ been very interested in the project.

14. He spent the second half of his life living in _____ remote village of Hogstail Common, _____ he wrote most of his novels.

15. _____ the time she retired, she _____ worked for the company for thirty two years, and during _____ time, she only took one or two days _____ sick.

16. I've _____ working on this essay _____ over a week, but _____ matter how much I work, I just can't seem to finish _____.

Exercise 2
Instructions as above.

1. Some people try to _____ up cigarettes by smoking _____ they feel sick, or by limiting themselves to one or _____ a day, but _____ methods are not very effective.

2. There were at _____ sixty people in the room, which was far _____ than the organizers expected, and _____ there were only 20 chairs, most of us _____ to stand.

3. I enjoy working _____ people who come _____ a wide range of backgrounds. _____ is the reason why I'm so keen _____ working for the U.N.

4. "Interphone", _____ is in _____ city center, is _____ of the biggest companies in _____ country.

5. Up _____ a few years ago, people _____ have the same career for life. Nowadays, _____ can reasonably expect _____ change careers two _____ three times.

6. In spite _____ being rather lazy, he is always able _____ get good results and has made _____ good impression _____ his tutors.

7. He spent _____ greater part of his life working _____ Barcelona, _____ he produced most of his most famous works of art.

8. _____ 2001 and 2004, unemployment figures dropped to an all-time low, but _____ 2004 to 2007 _____ rose _____ their highest level ever.

9. One _____ two of our lecturers commute from the country, but _____ of them live _____ the college or in the accommodations _____ the college provides.

10. Students are _____ allowed to miss a class _____ they inform their tutor at _____ three days in advance, _____ they are ill, in which case they should try to call the college on the day itself.

11. Please come _____ time to your lessons, and _____ prepared to work a _____ harder from _____ on.

12. We discussed holding the interviews _____ our Washington branch, but knowing how many people would apply _____ the job, we decided to use our bigger offices _____ New York.

13. In most respects he was a typical student, but _____ made him different _____ everybody else in his class _____ his enthusiasm for working _____ weekends.

14. I agree _____ I'm not perfect. I'm _____ capable _____ making mistakes as _____ else.

15. He approached his course _____ enthusiasm, _____ all the assignments he was set, and _____ excellent progress as a result.

Also see *Pronouns and determiners* on pages 46 – 47

Children and the family

Complete definitions 1 – 15 with words and expressions from the box. You will not need all of the words and expressions from the box.

> adolescence   adolescent   adopt   authoritarian   birth rate   bring up
> dependent   divorced   extended family   family life
> formative years   foster   foster child   foster family   freedom
> infancy   infant   juvenile   juvenile delinquency   lenient   minor (noun)   nuclear family
> nurture   over-protective   protective   raise   rebellious   relationship   relatives   responsible
> separated   siblings   single parent   single-parent family
> strict   supervision   running wild   teenager   upbringing   well-adjusted

1.   _____ is the period in someone's life when they change from being a child to being a young adult. A boy or a girl who is at this stage in their life is called an _____.

2.   A _____ is someone who has not reached the age at which they are legally an adult.

3.   Your brothers and sisters are sometimes referred to as your _____.

4.   A couple (for example, a husband and wife) who are _____ no longer live together. If a married couple get _____, their marriage is legally ended.

5.   A _____ is a family that looks after someone else's child in their own home for a period of time. A child who lives with this family is called a _____. The verb is _____.

6.   A _____ is a formal word for a young person, and can also be used as a word for a young person who has committed a crime.

7.   A _____ child is one who is mentally strong and able to deal with problems without becoming upset. A child who is badly behaved and refuses to obey his / her parents, teachers, etc., can be described as _____.

8.   Your _____ are those in your life when your character and beliefs are most strongly influenced.

9.   If you bring someone else's child into your family and legally make him or her your own child, we say that you _____ him / her.

10.   A _____ is a child between the ages of 13 and 19.

11.   An _____ is a baby or very young child. This period in a child's life is called _____.

12.   _____ and _____ both mean the same thing: to take care of children while they are growing up.

13.   An _____ is a family group that includes grandparents, aunts, uncles, etc. A _____ is a family unit consisting of a mother, a father, and their children.

14.   A _____ or _____ parent is one who makes their children follow rules and behave in a very "correct" way. The opposite of this is _____.

15.   A _____ is a child or other relative to whom you give food, money, and a home. This word can also be an adjective.

Exercise 2
Use your dictionary to check the meanings of the other words and expressions in the box.

Exercise 3
Complete this case study with appropriate words and expressions from the box in Exercise 1. You may need to change the form of some of the words.

Bob's problems began during his (1) _____. His parents got (2) _____ when he was young, and neither of his parents wanted to raise him or his brother and sister, so he was (3) _____ by a (4) _____ chosen by his parent's social worker. Unfortunately, his foster-father was a strict (5) _____ and often beat him. Bob rebelled against this strict (6) _____ and by the time he was eight, he was already (7) _____ stealing from shops and playing truant. By the time he reached (8) _____ sometime around his thirteenth birthday, he had already appeared in court several times, charged with (9) _____. The judge blamed his foster parents, explaining that children needed (10) _____ parents and guardians who would look after them properly. The foster father objected to this, pointing out that Bob's (11) _____ – his two brothers and sister – were (12) _____ children who behaved at home and worked well at school.

This has raised some interesting questions about the modern family system. While it is true that parents should not be too (13) _____ with children by letting them do what they want when they want, or be too (14) _____ by sheltering them from the realities of life, it is also true that they should not be too strict. It has also highlighted the disadvantages of the modern (15) _____ where the child has only its mother and father to rely on (or the (16) _____, in which the mother or father has to struggle particularly hard to support their (17) _____). In fact, many believe that we should return to traditional family values and the (18) _____ family: extensive research has shown that children from these families are generally better behaved and have a getter chance of success in later life.

Exercise 4
Now try this essay. Use words and expressions from the vocabulary box in Exercise 1, and any other words or expressions that you think would be relevant.

Some people believe that children nowadays have too much freedom. Others believe that children are protected too much by their parents. Which of these statements do you agree with? Use specific reasons and examples to support your decision.

Education

Exercise 1
Complete definitions 1 – 14 with words and expressions from the box. You will not need all of the words and expressions from the box.

> acquire   class   correspondence course   course   day release   degree
> discipline   doctorate   elementary (education)   elementary school
> enroll   exam   experience   faculty   fail   fees   grade   grades   grade school
> graduate (noun)   graduate (verb)   graduate school   grant   higher degree
> higher education   high school   junior high school   kindergarten   learn
> learning resources center   lecture   lecturer   lesson   literacy   mature (student)
> middle school   night class   numeracy   opportunity   pass   physical education
> private school   professor   prospectus   public school   qualifications   quarter
> retake (an exam)   resources   secondary (education)   semester   seminar
> SAT® (Scholastic Aptitude Test)   sit / take (an exam)   skills   study   subject
> syllabus   topic   tutor   tutorial   undergraduate

1.   A _____ is an educational course that you take at home, receiving your work and sending it back by mail or email. A _____ is a lesson in the evening for people who work during the day. People who have a job might be given _____ by their employer, which means that can take a day off work about once a week to attend a course of study.

2.   The _____ is an examination that students must take before they can go to university.

3.   A _____ is a period of time in which students are taught a subject in school (also called a _____.

4.   A _____ is a talk given to a group of students at college or university about a particular _____. The person who gives this talk is called a _____. A _____ is a meeting at which a group of students discuss something they are studying. A _____ is a meeting at which one student, or a small group of students, discusses something he / she is studying with his / her _____.

5.   _____ is the ability to read and write. _____ refers to basic skills in mathematics.

6.   A _____ is a small book that provides information about a university. Once a students who has read this book decides he / she would like to study there, he must _____ (in other words, he / she puts his / her name on the official list of students).

7.   A _____ is a main department at a university. This word can also be used to refer to the teaching staff of a school, college, university, etc.

8.   _____ refers to sports and exercise that children do at school as a school subject.

9.   A _____ is a school that is funded by taxes. A _____ is a school where the parents of the children who attend it must pay _____.

10.   A _____ is school for very young children (aged 4 or 5), which prepares them for the first _____ at school. An _____ is a school for the first six or eight years of a child's education. It is also known as a _____.

11.   A _____ is a list of the main subjects in a course of study (sometimes called a *curriculum*).

12.   A _____ is a school for students between the ages of 12 and 14 or 15. It is also known as
       a _____. From the age of 14 or 15, students attend a _____.

13.   A _____ is one of two periods into which the school year is divided. A _____ is
       one of four periods into which the school year is divided.

14.   A _____ is someone who has completed a course at school, college, or university. A
       _____ is a college or university where students can study for a _____ such as a
       Master's or Ph.D.

Exercise 2
Use your dictionary to check the meanings of the other words and expressions in the box.

Exercise 3
Complete this essay with appropriate words and expressions from the box in Exercise 1. You may
need to change the form of some of the words.

You are never too old to learn. Do you agree with this statement?

Education is a long process that not only provides us with basic (1) _____ such as
(2) _____ and (3) _____, but is also essential in shaping our future lives. From the moment
we enter (4) _____ as 5-year-olds, and as we progress through (5) _____ and
(6) _____ education, we are laying the foundations for the life ahead of us. We must
(7) _____ ourselves to work hard so that we can (8) _____ exams and gain the
(9) _____ we will need to secure a good job. We must also (10) _____ valuable life skills
so that we can fit in and work with those around us. And of course (11) _____ helps us to develop
our bodies and stay fit and healthy.

For most people, this process ends when they are in their mid-to-late teens and they (12 _____ from
high school. For others, however, it is the beginning of a lifetime of learning. After they finish school, many
progress to (13) _____ education where they will work towards a (14) _____ in a chosen
(15) _____ at university. After that, they may work for a while before opting to study at a
(16) _____ for a Masters degree, or a (17) _____. Alternatively, they may choose to attend
a (18) _____ after work or, if they have a sympathetic employer, obtain (19) _____ so that
they can study during the week. And if they live a long way from a college or university, they might follow a
(20) _____ using mail and the Internet. In fact, it is largely due to the proliferation of computers that
many people, who have not been near a school for many years, have started to study again and can proudly class
themselves as (21) _____ students.

We live in a fascinating and constantly changing world, and we must continually learn and acquire new
knowledge if we are to adapt and keep up with changing events. Our schooldays are just the beginning of this
process, and we should make the best of every (22) _____ to develop ourselves, whether we are
eighteen or eighty. You are, indeed, never too old to learn.

Exercise 4
Now try this essay. Use words and expressions from the vocabulary box in Exercise 1, and any other
words or expressions that you think would be relevant.

*Do you agree with this statement? "The most important things in life are not learnt at school or
college." Use examples and details in your answer.*

Food and diet

Complete definitions and sentences 1 – 12 with words and expressions from the box. You will not need all of the words and expressions from the box.

allergy   allergic   anorexia   balanced diet   bulimia   calcium   calories   carbohydrates   cholesterol   consume   consumption   diabetes   diet (noun + verb)   eating disorder   exercise   fast food   fat   fat farm   fiber   food group   food intolerance   food poisoning   free range   genetically modified (GM)   harvest   health food   heart disease   junk food   listeria   malnutrition   malnourished   minerals   monounsaturated   nutrition   nutritious   obese   obesity   organic   overweight   protein   salmonella   saturated   scarce   scarcity   underweight   vegan   veganism   vegetarian   vegetarianism   vitamins

1. _____ are the parts of fruit, vegetables and grains that your body cannot digest, and helps food to pass through your body. _____ is the oil found in food, and there are three main types of this: _____, polyunsaturated, and _____.

2. _____ are units used for measuring how much energy you get from food. _____ is a substance found in food such as eggs, milk, and meat that people need in order to grow and be healthy. _____ is a white chemical element that is an important part of bones and teeth, and is found in food products such as eggs, milk, and cheese. _____ are found in foods such as sugar, bread, and potatoes, and supply your body with heat and energy.

3. People who weigh more than they should often go on a _____ to help them lose weight. Some of them may go to a _____, an informal expression for a place where people can go to try to lose weight by eating in a healthy way and doing lots of _____.

4. _____ food is food which is produced without using artificial chemicals. _____ food is food produced from animals which are allowed to move around and feed naturally. _____ food is food that has been produced from a plant or animal that has had its gene structure changed in order to make it more productive or resistant to disease.

5. People who eat too much, or who don't eat enough (often because they think they look fat), suffer from a medical condition known generally as an _____. Examples of this include _____ and _____.

6. A _____ is someone who doesn't eat meat. A _____ is someone who doesn't eat meat or other products derived from animals (including cheese and milk).

7. _____ is food that is made very quickly, especially food like burgers and pizzas that you can take out. It is sometimes called _____, because it is often not very healthy or _____.

8. Someone who is heavier than they should be is _____. If they are a lot heavier than they should be, they are _____. The noun is _____. This can result in _____, cancer, _____, and many other serious illnesses.

9. E-coli, _____, and _____ are three kinds of _____.

10. Meat, vegetables, and dairy products are three of the main _____.

11. If you eat a _____, you eat the correct amounts of the right sorts of food; you do not eat too much of one particular sort of food.

12.   People who have a _____ are unable to eat certain kinds of food because it has a negative effect on them (although it will not affect them seriously). People with an _____ to certain kinds of food must avoid them, as the effects may be much more serious (for example, if someone who is _____ to peanuts eats something with peanuts in, it might kill them).

Exercise 2
Use your dictionary to check the meanings of the other words and expressions in the box.

Exercise 3
Complete this essay with appropriate words and expressions from the box in Exercise 1. You may need to change the form of some of the words.

"Despite the huge variety of foods in our supermarkets, it is becoming increasingly difficult to eat a healthy diet. Do you agree? Support your opinion by using specific reasons and examples."

Most children enjoy eating (1) _____, but scientific tests have shown us that burgers and pizzas can lack essential (2) _____ and (3) _____ which are essential for health and growth, while simultaneously containing large amounts of (4) _____ and (5) _____ which can result in obesity and heart problems. Many children end up suffering from (6) _____, since they eat too much of the wrong sort of food. In fact, in many areas of the developed world, a lot of children show similar symptoms to those in poorer developing countries, where (7) _____ of food causes thousands of deaths from starvation, especially in the wake of natural disasters which ruin crops and in some cases totally destroy the annual (8) _____.

Dieticians tell us that we must eat a (9) _____, as it is essential we consume sufficient quantities of the different food groups. They tell us that we should all eat more (10) _____, which cannot be digested by the body, and fewer foods which are high in (11) _____, as this can block the walls of arteries and lead to heart problems. This is good advice, of course, but our lifestyles often make this difficult. Many of the ready-prepared foods we buy from supermarkets are high in (12) _____, giving us more energy than we actually need. (13) _____ foods are appearing on our supermarket shelves, even though nobody is really sure if altering the composition of food cells is safe. We have the option, of course, of buying (14) _____ foods, but naturally-cultivated fruits and vegetables are expensive. And to make matters worse, we are continually hearing about outbreaks of (15) _____ and (16) _____ which put us off eating certain foods, as nobody wants to spend time in hospital suffering from (17) _____.

A few things to watch out for next time you go shopping. If you have the time and the money, that is!

Exercise 4
Now try this essay. Use words and expressions from the vocabulary box in Exercise 1, and any other words or expressions that you think would be relevant.

"If food tastes good, it's probably bad for you". How far do you agree with this statement? Use specific reasons and examples to support your opinion.

The media

Exercise 1

Complete sentences and definitions 1 – 12 with words and expressions from the box. You will not need all of the words and expressions.

airtime   audience   broadcast   broadsheet   censor   censorship   channel check book journalism   circulation   current affairs   coverage   documentary   download dumbing down   editor   entertainment   exploit   feature   freedom of the press gutter press   honest   information   informed   Internet   invasion of privacy   journalism journalist   libel   libelous   log on   mass media   media circus   media event media tycoon   news   online   paparazzi   the press   program   read between the lines readership   reality TV   reporter   restriction   slander   slanderous   tabloid   tabloid TV   the Internet   unscrupulous   website

1. _____ is the crime of saying something about someone that is not true and is likely to damage their reputation (the adjective is _____). _____ is the illegal act of writing things about someone that are not true (the adjective is _____).

2. If you _____, you guess something that is not expressed directly (for example, if a newspaper reports a story, it might not tell you the truth or give you all the information you want, so you try to guess what that information is).

3. _____ is an occasion when someone finds out or uses information about your private life, especially illegally.

4. A _____ is a newspaper that is printed on large sheets of paper, and usually contains serious news. A _____ is a newspaper that is printed on smaller sheets of paper and generally contains stories about famous people (papers like these are sometimes referred to as the _____, because many of the stories and either untrue, or are about sex and crime). _____ refers to television programs that are intended to be shocking or exciting.

5. If a media company is accused of _____ its stories or programs, it means that it presents these stories or programs in a simple and attractive way without giving many details.

6. A _____ is someone who writes news reports for newspapers, television, etc. A _____ often does the same thing, and then tells people the news himself / herself (for example, by appearing on a television program).

7. The process of removing parts of books, films, letters, etc., that are considered unsuitable for moral, religious, or political reasons is called _____.

8. A _____ is someone who owns and controls several different newspapers, television stations, etc., and is very rich as a result.

9. _____ programs are television programs in which ordinary people are put into artificially created environments and situations in order to entertain people (the most famous example is "Big Brother").

10. A _____ is a radio or television program that deals with real people, events, places, etc., and is designed to inform people about different things. A _____ program is one that deals mainly with political, social, and economic events that are happening now.

11. _____ is the practice of paying people a lot of money for information that can be used in newspaper stories, especially stories about crime or famous people.

12. _____ refers to the amount of time given to someone or something in a radio or television broadcast. _____ refers to the amount of attention that television, radio, and newspapers give to something, or to the way in which something is reported. A newspaper's _____ is the group or number of people who read that newspaper.

Exercise 2
Use your dictionary to check the meanings of the other words and expressions in the box.

Exercise 3
Complete this essay with appropriate words and expressions from the box in Exercise 1. You may need to change the form of some of the words.

"The media plays a valuable role in keeping us informed and entertained. However, many people believe it has too much power and freedom". Do you agree?'

Barely a hundred years ago, if we wanted to stay (1) _____ about what was going on in the world, we had to rely on word of mouth or, at best, newspapers. But because communication technology was very basic, the news we received was often days or weeks old.

We still have newspapers, of course, but they have changed almost beyond recognition. Whether we choose to read the (2) _____, with their quality (3) _____ of news and other (4) _____ by top (5) _____ and acclaimed (6) _____ or if we prefer the popular (7) _____, with their lively gossip and colorful stories, we are exposed to a wealth of information barely conceivable at the beginning of the last century.

We also have television and radio. News (8) _____ let us know about world events practically as they happen, while sitcoms, chat shows, and (9) _____, etc., keep us entertained and informed. And there is also the (10) _____, where we can access information from millions of (11) _____ around the world which we can then (12) _____ onto our own computers.

However, these forms of (13) _____ and (14) _____ (or "infotainment" as they are now sometimes collectively called) have their negative side. Famous personalities frequently accuse the (15) _____ (and sometimes even respectable papers) of (16) _____by camera-wielding (17) _____ who are determined to get a picture or a story regardless of who they upset. Newspapers are often accused of (18)_____ by angry politicians who dislike reading lies about themselves, and there are frequent accusations of (19) _____, with (20) _____ newspapers paying people lots of money for stories about crime and famous people. Of course, it is not just the papers which are to blame. Sex and violence are increasing on the television, and many complain that there is increased (21) _____ of news and current affairs programs, with major stories being presented in a simple and attractive way, but with very little detail. Others argue that too much time is being given to (22) _____ shows, in which ordinary people are put into artificially created environments and situations for our entertainment. Meanwhile, anyone with a computer can go (23) _____ to find undesirable material placed there by equally undesirable people.

Some people argue that the government should impose stricter (24) _____ to prevent such things happening. But others argue that (25) _____ and media is the keystone of a free country. Personally, I take the view that while the media may occasionally abuse its position of power, the benefits greatly outweigh the disadvantages. Our lives would be much emptier without the wealth of information available to us today, and perhaps we are better people as a result.

Exercise 4
Now try this essay. Use words and expressions from the box in Exercise 1, and any other words or expressions that you think would be relevant.

What are the qualities or features of a good newspaper, current affairs television program, or news website? Use specific details and examples to explain your answer.

Money and finance

Complete sentences and paragraphs 1 – 20 with a word or expression from the box. In each case, the word / expression you need is connected in some way with the word in **bold** in the same sentence / paragraph (for example, it might have a similar meaning, it might be an opposite, or it might be a word that is sometimes confused with that word). In some cases you might need to change the form of the word in the box.

> balance   bank   bankrupt   bargain   bill   borrow   broke   bankrupt   cash   check
> cost of living   credit card   credit   debt   debit   deposit   discount
> distribution of wealth   dividends   economical   economize   exorbitant   expenditure
> extravagant   frugal   income   income tax   inflation   inherit   insolvent   interest
> in the black   in the red   invest   investment   invoice   lend   loan   loss   market
> mortgage   on credit   overcharged   overdraft   overpriced   pension   priceless   profit
> receipt   reduction   refund   salary   save   savings and loan association
> shares   statement   stocks   tax / rent (etc) rebate   undercharged
> unemployment / housing / child (etc.) welfare   wage   wealthy   welfare   withdraw   worthless

1.   **Income** is the money you receive (your *wage* or *salary* is part of your income), and _____ refers to the money you spend.

2.   If you **lend** money, you let someone use your money for a certain period of time. If you _____ money, you take someone's money for a short time, and then you pay it back.

3   A **discount** is the percentage by which a full price is reduced in a store. A _____ is money paid back to a customer when, for example, they return something to a store.

4.   If a person or company is **insolvent**, they have lost all their money. If a person or company is _____, they have lost all their money, have then borrowed a lot, and cannot pay it back.

5.   A bank **statement** is a detailed written document from a bank showing how much money has gone into and come out of a bank account. A _____ is the amount of money you have in your bank account.

6.   If your bank account is **in the red**, the amount of money you have spent is greater than the money you have made, and so you have less than $0 in your bank account. If your account is _____, you have more than $0 in your bank account.

7.   An **invoice** is a note, or *bill*, sent to you to ask for payment for goods or services, and a _____ is a note (from a store, for example) which shows how much you have paid for something.

8.   When you make a **profit**, you gain money from selling something which is more than the money you paid for it. When you make a _____, you have spent money which you have not gotten back.

9.   Something which is **overpriced** is too expensive. Something which is _____ costs much more than its true value.

10.   If you **save** money, you keep it so that you can use it later. If you _____ money, you put it into property, stocks, etc., so that it will increase in value.

11. A **wage** and a _____ are both money you receive for doing a job, but the first is usually paid *daily* or *weekly* and the second is usually paid *monthly*.

12. A **worthless** object is something which has no value. A _____ object is an extremely valuable object.

13. If you **deposit** money in an account, you put money into the account. If you _____ money, you take it out of your account.

14. If you have been **undercharged**, you have paid less than you should have for goods or services. If you have been _____, you have paid too much.

15. **Extravagant** describes someone who spends a lot of money. _____ describes someone who is careful with money.

16. A **bill** is a piece of paper showing the amount of money that you have to pay for goods or services. A _____ is the same thing, but shows what you have to pay after a meal in a restaurant.

17. When you **credit** an account, you put money into it. When you _____ an account, you take money out of it.

18. A **bank** is a business which holds money for its clients, and deals with money generally. A _____ is similar, but is usually used by people who want to save money, or to borrow money to buy a house.

19. A **loan** is money that you borrow from a bank to buy something. A _____ is similar, but in this case the money is only used to buy property.

20. A **loan** is money that you borrow from a bank, where a formal arrangement has been made with the bank to borrow it. An _____ is the amount of money that you take out of your bank account, which is more than there is in your account. It is usually done without making a formal arrangement with your bank.

Exercise 2
Use your dictionary to check the meanings of the other words and expressions in the box. Note that many of them can have more than one grammatical function without changing their form (for example, *balance* can be a noun and a verb). Also note that some of the words can have more than one meaning (for example, a *bill* is a banknote, and it is also a piece of paper showing you how much you have to pay for a product or service).

Exercise 3
Complete this conversation with appropriate words and expressions from the box in Exercise 1. You may need to change the form of some of the words.

"Financial advice from a father to a son"

In the play "Hamlet" by William Shakespeare, a father gives his son some financial advice. "Neither a borrower nor a lender be", he says. He is trying to tell his son that he should never (1) _____ money from anyone because it will make it difficult for him to manage his finances. Likewise he should never give a (2) _____ to a friend because he will probably never see the money again, and will probably lose his friend as well.

91

The play was written over four hundred years ago, but today many parents would give similar advice to their children. Imagine the conversation they would have now:

Jim: Right dad, I'm off to college now.

Dad: All right son, but let me give you some sound financial advice before you go.

Jim: Oh come on dad…..

Dad: Now listen, this is important. The first thing you should do is to make sure you balance your (3) _____ – the money you receive from me and mom – and your (4) _____ – the money you spend. If you spend too much, you will end up with an (5) _____ at the bank. Don't expect me to pay it for you.

Jim: But it's so difficult. Things are so expensive, and the (6) _____ goes up all the time. (7) _____ is running at about 10%.

Dad: I know, but you should try to (8) _____. Avoid expensive stores and restaurants. Also, leave your money in a good local (9) _____ account . They offer a much higher rate of (10) _____ than banks. Also, avoid buying things (11) _____.

Jim: Why?

Dad: Because some stores charge you an (12) _____ amount of money to buy things over a period of time. It's much better to (13) _____ a little bit of money each week so that when you see something you want, you can buy it outright. Try to wait for the sales, when stores offer huge (14) _____ and you can pick up a (15) _____. And try to get a (16) _____.

Jim: How do I do that?

Dad: Easy. When you buy something, ask the store if they'll lower the price by, say, 10%. Next, when you eventually get a job and are earning a good salary, try to (17) _____ the money in a good company. Buy (18) _____ in government organizations or (19) _____ in private companies.

Jim: OK dad, I've heard enough. Thanks for the advice. It's been (20) _____.

Dad: Well, it's true what they say: there are some things that money just can't buy.

Exercise 4
Now try this essay. Use words and expressions from the box in Exercise 1, and any other words or expressions that you think would be relevant.

Some people say that "Money makes the world go round"; others say that "Money is the root of all evil". Which of these do you agree with? Use examples and details in your answer.

Nature and the environment

Exercise 1

Replace the words and expressions in **bold** in sentences 1 – 15 with one of those from the box. You will not need all of the words and expressions from the box.

acid rain	activists	animal rights	battery farming	biodegradable packaging	biodiversity
biofuels	breeding	(in) captivity	CFC gases	climate change	conservation
conservation program	conserve	contaminated	deforestation	degradation	desertification
eco-friendly	ecological	ecology	ecosystem	emissions	endangered species
environmentalists	environmentally friendly	erosion	extinct		
fossil fuels	fumes	genetically modified	global warming	green belt	greenhouse effect
greenhouse gases	intensive farming	natural behavior	natural resources	organic	
organic farming	ozone-friendly	ozone layer	poaching	pollute	(air) pollution
rare breeds	rainforest	recycle	recycling	renewable / sustainable energy	research
solar power	tidal energy	toxic waste	unleaded gas	wildlife management	

1.   In some countries, building is restricted or completely banned in the **area of farmland or woods and parks which surround a community**.

2.   More and more companies are **using boxes, cartons, and cans which can easily be decomposed by organisms such as bacteria, or by sunlight, sea, water, etc.,** for their products.

3.   The burning of some fuels creates **carbon dioxide, carbon monoxide, sulfur dioxide, and methane** which rise into the atmosphere.

4.   Farmers have cleared acres of **thick wooded land in tropical regions where the precipitation is very high** to provide pasture for their cattle.

5.   Planting trees and bushes can provide some protection from **the gradual wearing away of soil**.

6.   We should all try to **process waste material so that it can be used again**.

7.   Many shops now sell fruit and vegetables which are **cultivated naturally, without using any chemical fertilizers or pesticides**.

8.   This bread is made from wheat which has been **altered at a molecular level so as to change certain characteristics which can be inherited**.

9.   Most modern cars use **fuel which has been made without lead additives**.

10. **Polluted precipitation which kills trees** often falls a long distance from the source of the pollution.

11. Human activity has had a devastating effect on the **living things, both large and small**, in many parts of the word.

12. The **gases and other substances** which come from factories using oil, coal, and other **fuels which are the remains of plants and animals** can cause serious damage to the environment.

13. Don't drink that water. It's been **made dirty by something being added to it**.

14. Friends of the Earth, Greenpeace, and other **people concerned with protecting the environment** are holding an international summit in Geneva next month.

15. **The heating up of the earth's atmosphere by pollution** is threatening life as we know it.

Use your dictionary to check the meanings of the other words and expressions in the box.

Exercise 3
Read this essay and complete the gaps with one of the words or expressions from the box in Exercise 1.

"Environmental degradation is a major world problem. What causes this problem, and what can we do to prevent it?"

There is no doubt that the environment is in trouble. Factories burn (1) _____ which produce (2) _____ , and this kills trees. At the same time, (3) _____ rise into the air and contribute to (4) _____ which threatens to melt the polar ice cap. Meanwhile farmers clear huge areas of (5) _____ in places such as the Amazon to produce feeding land for cattle or produce wood for building. Rivers and oceans are so heavily (6) _____ by industrial waste that it is no longer safe to go swimming. Cars pump out poisonous (7) _____which we all have to breathe in. (8) _____ and overfishing are killing off millions of animals, including whales, elephants, and other (9) _____ In fact, all around us, all living things large and small which comprise our finely balanced (10) _____ are being systematically destroyed by human greed and thoughtlessness.

There is a lot we can all do, however, to help prevent this. The easiest thing, of course, is to (11) _____ waste material such as paper and glass so that we can use it again. We should also check that the things we buy from supermarkets are packaged in (12) _____ which decomposes easily. At the same time, we should make a conscious effort to avoid foods which are (13) _____ (at least until someone proves that they are safe both for us and for the environment). If you are truly committed to protecting the environment, of course, you should only buy (14) _____fruit and vegetables, safe in the knowledge that they have been naturally cultivated. Finally, of course, we should buy a small car that uses (15) _____ which is less harmful to the environment or, even better, make more use of public transportation.

The serious (16) _____, however, do much more. They are aware of the global issues involved and will actively involve themselves in (17) _____ by making sure our forests are kept safe for future generations. They will oppose activities which are harmful to animals, such as (18) _____. And they will campaign to keep the (19) _____ around our towns and cities free from new building.

We cannot all be as committed as them, but we can at least do our own little bit at grass roots level. We, as humans, have inherited the earth, but that doesn't mean we can do whatever we like with it.

Exercise 4
Now try this essay. Use words and expressions from Exercise 1, and any other words or expressions that you think would be relevant.

Some people think that the government should spend as much money as possible on protecting the environment. Others think this money should be spent on other things such as education and healthcare. Which one of these opinions do you agree with? Use specific reasons and details to support your answer.

Exercise 1

Some of the words and expressions from the box below have been defined in sentences 1 – 16. In some cases, these definitions are <u>correct</u>, and in some they are <u>wrong</u>. Decide which are which.

---

accelerate   accident   accident risk   auto theft   back out   black spot   brake   congestion
crosswalk   cut in (in a vehicle)   cycle lane   destination   dominate
drunk driving   driver   driver's licence   driving test   expressway   fatalities   a fine   freeway
gas   highway   highway patrol   injuries   intersection   interstate   joyriding   mile
mobility   overtake   park and ride   pedestrian   pedestrian mall   pollution
public transportation   pull in   pull over   road rage   road work   rush hour   safety island
sidewalk   to speed   speed limit   subsidized (e.g., public transportation)   to tailgate
traffic light / signal   traffic calming   traffic circle / rotary   traffic-free zone   traffic jam
traffic school   transport strategy   turnpike

1.　**Rush hour** is the time of day when there are not many vehicles on the road because most people are at home.

2.　If a service such as public transportation is **subsidized**, all of its running costs are paid for by the government or a local authority.

3.　A **traffic school** is a school for people who want to learn to drive a motor vehicle.

4.　An **expressway** is a wide road (usually in a city) where people can drive quickly, and is the U.S. equivalent of a British *dual carriageway*.

5.　**Road rage** is anger or violent behavior by one driver toward another driver.

6.　**Traffic calming** measures are fines and other penalties imposed by the police on bad or dangerous drivers.

7.　In the U.S.A., the **interstate** is part of the national public transportation system (including trains and buses) which people use to travel around the country.

8.　Someone who has been accused of **joyriding** has stolen a car in order to drive it for pleasure, usually in a dangerous way.

9.　A **turnpike** is a main road in the eastern part of the U.S.A. that drivers must pay to use.

10.　Someone who **backs out** in a vehicle drives it very quickly and dangerously, usually in a busy or built-up area.

11.　A **cycle lane** is a part of the road that is set aside for people on bicycles, and which may not be used by drivers of motor vehicles.

12.　A **traffic-free zone** is a main road between major towns and cities that drivers do not have to pay to use.

13.　**Fatalities** (in this context) refers to people who are injured in accidents on the road.

14.　A **black spot** is a place on a road where a lot of car accidents happen.

15.　A **mile** is a measure of distance equivalent to 1.609 kilometers.

16.　A **sidewalk** is a part of the road in a town or city where drivers can park their vehicle.

Exercise 2
Use your dictionary to check the meanings of the other words and expressions in the box.

Exercise 3
Complete this article with appropriate words and expressions from the box in Exercise 1. You may need to change the form of some of the words.

---

(1) _____ and (2) _____ on our roads are increasing from year to year: last year, 2,827 people were killed and almost 300,000 hurt in traffic-related accidents in the state. Most of these were caused by drivers (3) _____ in built-up areas, where many seem to disregard the 30mph (4) _____, or (5) _____, especially around July 4th and Thanksgiving, when more alcohol is consumed than at any other time. In many cases, it is (6) _____ who are the victims, knocked down as they are walking across the street at (7) _____ by drivers who seem to have forgotten that a red (8) _____ means "Stop".

But these innocent victims, together with the help of the highway patrol and local safety groups, are fighting back. In New Stockholm, a city plagued by (9) _____ and (10) _____ caused by traffic, and a notorious accident (11) _____ for pedestrians and cyclists, the city council has recently implemented its new (12) _____, which has improved the flow of traffic to the benefit of those on foot or on two wheels. (13) _____ measures such as speed bumps have slowed traffic down. (14) _____ programs have helped reduce the number of cars in the city, as office workers and shoppers leave their cars outside the city and bus in instead. Harley Street, the main shopping thoroughfare, has been designated a (15) _____, closed to all vehicles during the day. There are more (16) _____ on main routes into the city, making it safer for the huge number of students and residents who rely on bicycles to get around. And (17) _____ public transportation has helped to keep down the cost of using buses. Meanwhile, the police and the courts are coming down hard on drivers who misuse the roads, handing down large (18) _____ or even jail sentences on selfish, inconsiderate drivers who believe it is their right to (19) _____ the roads; for these people, (20) _____ is not offered as a softer alternative.

Exercise 4
Now try this essay. Use words and expressions from the box in Exercise 1, and any other words or expressions that you think would be relevant.

Do you agree or disagree with the following statement?: It is time we all relied less on private motor vehicles to get around, and instead used other forms of transport. Use specific examples and details to support your answer.

Science and technology

Exercise 1

Complete definitions 1 – 15 with words and expressions from the box. You will not need all of the words and expressions from the box.

analyze   bioclimatology   biology   breakthrough   cellphone   chemistry
computers   control   cryogenics   cybernetics   development   digital   discover   discovery
e-mail   experiment   genetic engineering   genetic fingerprinting
genetic modification   geneticist   information superhighway   information technology (IT)
innovation   Internet   invent   invention   life expectancy   microchip   modified
molecular biology   nuclear engineering   physics   research   safeguard
scientist   technocrat   technologist   technophile   technophobe

1. _____ is the practice or science of changing the genes of a living thing, especially in order to make it more suitable for a particular purpose.

2. A _____ is a rule, law, or plan that protects people or something from harm or problems.

3. _____ is the study of living things.

4. A _____ is someone who does not like, trust, or want to use technology, especially computers.

5. A _____ is a discovery or achievement that comes after a lot of hard work.

6. _____ is the study or use of computers and electronic systems for storing and using information.

7. If something is _____, it is changed slightly in order to improve it.

8. A _____ is a scientist who studies or works in genetics.

9. _____ is the use of technology to make copies of natural things (for example, artificial body parts).

10. A _____ is a scientist or other technical expert with a high position in industry or government.

11. _____ is the detailed study of something in order to discover new facts.

12. _____ is the science that studies the effects of low temperatures, especially the use of low temperatures for preserving the bodies of dead people.

13. An _____ is a scientific test to find out what happens to someone or something in particular conditions.

14. _____ is the length of time that someone is likely to live.

15. _____ is the invention or use of new ideas, methods, equipment, etc.

Use your dictionary to check the meanings of the other words and expressions in the box.

Exercise 3
Complete this essay with appropriate words and expressions from the box in Exercise 1. You may need to change the form of some of the words.

"Science and technology have come a long way in the last 60 years, and our lives have become better as a result. Do you agree with this statement?"

The second half of the twentieth century saw more changes than in the previous two hundred years. Penicillin has already been (1) _____ and used to treat infections; there have been many remarkable advances in medicine that have helped to increase our average (2) _____ way beyond that of our ancestors. Incredible (3) _____ such as television have changed the way we spend our leisure hours. Perhaps the most important (4) _____, however, has been the microchip. Nobody could have imagined, when it was first (5) _____, that within a matter of years, this tiny piece of silicon and circuitry would be found in almost every household object from the kettle to the DVD recorder. And nobody could have predicted the sudden proliferation of computers that would completely change our lives, allowing us to access information from the other side of the world via the (6) _____ or send messages around the world by (7) _____ at the touch of a button. Meanwhile, (8) _____ into other aspects of information technology is making it easier and cheaper for us to talk to friends and relations around the world. Good news for (9) _____ who love modern technology, bad news for the (10) _____ who would prefer to hide from these modern miracles.

But everything has a price. The development of (11) _____ led to mass automation in factories, which in turn led to millions losing their jobs. The genius of Einstein led to the horrors of the atomic bomb and the dangerous uncertainties of (12) _____ (we hear of accidents and mishaps at nuclear power stations around the world, where (13) _____ to prevent accidents were inadequate). The relatively new science of (14) _____ has been seen as a major step forward, but putting modified foods onto the market before scientists had properly (15) _____ them was perhaps one of the most irresponsible decisions of the 1990s. Meanwhile, pharmaceutical and cosmetic companies continue to (16) _____ on animals, a move that many consider to be cruel and unnecessary.

Of course we all rely on modern science and technology to improve our lives. However, we need to make sure that we (17) _____ it rather than the other way round.

Exercise 4
Now try this essay. Use words and expressions from the box in Exercise 1, and any other words or expressions that you think would be relevant.

What, in your opinion, has been the single most important scientific or technological development of the last fifty years? Use specific reasons and details to support your answer.

Town and country

Exercise 1

Complete sentences 1 – 12 with a word or expression from the box. Then take the letter indicated at the end of each sentence, and write it in the grid that follows the sentences. If you do this correctly, you will "find" another word which means *"showing the influence of many different countries and cultures"*.

> agriculture   amenities   apartment block   arable land   atmosphere
> to breed crime   building sites   Central Business District (CBD)   commute   commuter
> commuter belt   congestion   construction   cost of living   crops   crowded   cultivation
> cultural events   depopulation   development   drug abuse   employment   environment
> facilities   fields   green belt   industry   infrastructure   housing project   inner city   lively
> mall / shopping mall   melting pot   metropolis   migration   nature   nightlife   outskirts
> peaceful   peak period   pedestrian precinct   pollution   population   population explosion
> poverty   productive land   property prices   prospects   resident   residential area   rural
> rush hour   slum   street crime   stressful   suburbs   traffic jam   unemployment   urban
> urban lifestyle   urban sprawl

1. If the town in which you live offers you good _____, it offers you the chance for success, especially in a job or career. (*Write the 7th letter of this word in the grid*)

2. A _____ is a big city, especially one that is busy and exciting. (*Write the 5th letter of this word in the grid*)

3. An _____ is the set of systems within a place or organization that affect how well it operates (for example, a public transportation system or road system). (*Write the 6th letter of this word in the grid*)

4. A _____ is someone who travels regularly to and from work. (*Write the 3rd letter of this word in the grid*)

5. The _____ of a town or city are the areas that are furthest away from the center. (*Write the 1st letter of this word in the grid*)

6. _____ is a situation in which many people leave a place in order to live somewhere else. (*Write the 3rd letter of this word in the grid*)

7. _____ occurs when there are a lot of vehicles on the road, and as a result the traffic moves very slowly. (*Write the 2nd letter of this word in the grid below*)

8. If a town or city is described as a _____, it has people of many different races, religions, cultures, etc., living together. (*2 words: Write the 3rd letter of the 1st word in the grid*)

9. _____ refers to the movement of people from one place to another (often from one part of a country to another, or from one country to another country). (*Write the 2nd letter of this word in the grid*)

10. If a situation, place, etc., is _____, it causes a lot of pressure and makes people worry. (*Write the 2nd letter of this word in the grid*)

11. _____ is an adjective relating to towns and cities. (*Write the 4th letter of this word in the grid*)

12. A town's _____ are the things that make it comfortable and pleasant to live in (for example, parks, theaters, stores, etc.). (*Write the 4th letter of this word in the grid*)

Sentence number:	1	2	3	4	5	6	7	8	9	10	11	12
Letter:												

Exercise 2

Use your dictionary to check the meanings of the other words and expressions in the box.

Exercise 3

Complete this essay with appropriate words and expressions from Exercise 1. You may need to change the form of some of the words, and one of the words you will need is the extra word you revealed by doing Exercise 1.

"Describe a place where you live or have lived, outlining its good points and bad points".

For seven years I lived in Singapore, a (1) _____ of almost three million people. Like London, Paris, and New York, Singapore is a (2) _____ city, with people from different parts of the world living and working together. I enjoyed the (3) _____ lifestyle I led there, and made the most of the superb (4) _____, ranging from the excellent stores to some of the best restaurants in the world. In the evenings and at weekends there were always (5) _____: with such diverse attractions as classical western music, an exhibition of Malay art, or a Chinese opera in the street, it was difficult to get bored. Perhaps most impressive, however, was the remarkable transportation (6) _____, with excellent roads, a swift and efficient bus service, and a state-of-the-art subway system which could whisk (7) _____ from the suburbs straight into the heart of the city (this was particularly important, as the government banned private cars from entering the (8) _____ during the morning and afternoon (9) _____ in order to reduce (10) _____ on the roads and (11) _____ from the exhausts).

Of course, living in a city like this has its disadvantages as well. For a start, the (12) _____ can be very high – renting an apartment, for example, is very expensive. And as the city is expanding, there are a lot of (13) _____ where new apartments are continually being built to deal with the (14) _____ which is a direct result of the government encouraging people to have more children.

Fortunately, Singapore doesn't suffer from problems that are common in many cities such as (15) _____, which is partly the result of the government imposing very severe penalties on anyone bringing narcotics into the country, so it is safe to walk the streets at night. In fact, the (16) _____ housing estates there are probably the safest and most orderly in the world.

Singapore wouldn't be ideal for everyone, however, especially if you come from the countryside and are used to a (17) _____ lifestyle. The traditional villages that were once common have disappeared as the residents there realised there were no (18) _____ for their future and moved into new government housing in the city. Nowadays, there is very little (19) _____ around the city, which means that Singapore imports almost all of its food. And despite a "green" approach to city planning, the (20) _____ which has eaten into the countryside has had a detrimental effect on the (21) _____.

Exercise 4

Now try this essay. Use words and expressions from Exercise 1, and any other words or expressions that you think would be relevant.

Some people prefer to live in the countryside or in a small town. Others prefer to live in a big city. Which place would you prefer to live in? Use specific reasons and details to support your answer.

Travel

Exercise 1

Look at the words and expressions in the box, then answer questions 1 – 16. Some of these questions ask you to explain what a word or expression means, and some of them ask you to complete a sentence with the appropriate word(s) or expression(s).

> acclimatize   alien   all-inclusive   business class   check-in
> check in (to a hotel or for a flight)   check out (of a hotel)   coach class   consulate   cruise
> culture shock   customs   deport   disembark   displaced   economic migrants   ecotourism
> embark   embassy   emigrate   emigration   excursion   expatriate
> first class   flight   gate   green card   illegal alien   immigrant   immigration
> independent traveler   internally displaced   journey   long-haul   luggage   mass tourism
> migrant   migrate   package tour   package tourist   passport   persona non grata   refugee
> repatriate   safari   short-haul   tour operator   trafficking   travel agency   travel agent   trip
> UNHCR   visa   voyage   work permit

1. What does the expression *persona non grata* mean?

2. Complete this sentence: _____ is the nervous or confused feeling that people sometimes get when they arrive in a place that is very different from the place they normally live.

3. What is the difference between a *travel agency* and a *tour operator*?

4. Complete this sentence: An _____ is a short trip somewhere, usually for one day or part of a day.

5. Complete this sentence: A _____ seat is the cheapest type of seat on a plane or train. The most expensive type of seat is called _____. Between these two, there is _____.

6. Would you be happy if the country that you were staying in *deported* you?

7. Complete this sentence: _____ refers to the large numbers of people that travel for their vacation, usually over long distances.

8. What is the difference between a *package tourist* and an *independent traveler*?

9. Is a *refugee* the same as an *expatriate*?

10. What do you think the letters *UNHCR* stand for?

11. Complete this sentence: _____ is the business of creating and selling vacations that give people the chance to learn about a natural environment, and which cause little damage to the environment itself.

12. If someone has been *repatriated*, what has happened to them?

13. What is a *cruise*? What is a *safari*?

14. Why might someone want a *green card*?

15. If someone is *trafficking* something, are they doing something that is legal or something that is illegal?

16. Complete this sentence: A person who has been _____ has been forced to move from one part of their country to another (often because of a war or other threatening situation).

Exercise 2
Use your dictionary to check the meanings of the other words and expressions in the box.

Exercise 3
Read this essay and complete the gaps with one of the words or expressions from the box in Exercise 1. You may need to change the form of some of the words.

"There are two types of traveler: those who do it because they *want* to, and those who do it because they *have* to. Discuss this statement, using specific examples".

Most of us have, at some point in our lives, experienced the joys of travel. We go to the (1) _____ to pick up our brochures. We book a two-week (2) _____ with flights and accommodations included, (or if we are (3) _____, we make our own way to the country and travel around from place to place with a rucksack on our back). We make sure we have all the right currency, our passport, and any (4) _____ that are necessary to get us into the country. We go to the airport and (5) _____. We strap ourselves into our tiny (6) _____ aircraft seats and a few hours later we (7) _____ from the aircraft, strange new sights, smells, and sounds greeting us. Nowadays, it seems, the whole world goes on vacation at once: the age of (8) _____ is in full swing!

But for the great majority of people around the world, travel is done in the face of great adversity and hardship. They never get to indulge in an (9) _____ vacation in a luxury hotel with all meals and drinks included. They never get to explore the lush Amazon rain forest or the frozen wastes of the Arctic on an (10) _____ vacation. For them, travel is a matter of life and death. I refer, of course, to all the (11) _____ escaping from their own countries, or the (12) _____, moved from one part of their country to another by an uncaring government, or (13) _____ forced to find a job and seek a living wherever they can.

Can you imagine anything worse than the misery these people must face? Let's not confuse them with those (14) _____, who choose to live in another country and often have nice houses and high salaries. These people are simply desperate to survive. As well as losing their homes because of war or famine or other natural disasters, they must come to terms with their new environment: for many, the (15) _____ can be too great. And while many countries with an open policy on (16) _____ will welcome them in with open arms, others will simply turn them away. These people become (17) _____, unwanted and unwelcome. Even if they manage to get into a country, they will often be (18) _____ or repatriated. Their future is uncertain.

Something to think about, perhaps, the next time you are (19) _____ to your five-star hotel by a palm-fringed beach or sitting in a coach on an (20) _____to a pretty castle in the countryside.

Exercise 4
Now try this essay. Use words and expressions from the box in Exercise 1, and any other words or expressions that you think would be relevant.

What are the good things and bad things about traveling? Use specific examples to explain your answer.

Exercise 1

Look at the words and expressions in the box, and answer questions 1 – 14. You may need to change the form of some of the words.

> adverse working conditions   applicant   application form   be laid off
> blue-collar worker   boss   candidate   commission   demanding   dismiss   dismissal
> downsize   employee   employer   fire   fixed income   flexible working hours   freelance
> full time   hire   homeworker   incentives   incentive scheme   income   increment
> interview   interviewee   interviewer   job satisfaction   job security   manager
> manual worker   manufacturing industry   (on) leave   overtime   part-time   pension
> pension contributions   perks   profession   promotion   raise   recruitment drive
> repetitive strain injury (RSI)   resign   retire   rewards and benefits   salary   self-employed
> semi-skilled   service industry   sick building syndrome   sickness benefit   skilled
> a steady job   stress   supervisor   unemployed   unemployment   union   unskilled
> unsociable hours   wage   (on) welfare   white-collar worker   workaholic

1. Replace the word in **bold** in this sentence with another word from the box which has a similar meaning: "A lot of people wanted the job, but she was the best **candidate**".

2. What is the difference between a *wage* and a *salary*?

3. Complete this sentence: _____ is a painful condition of the muscles in the hands and the arms caused by doing the same movement many times (for example, using a computer over a long period of time).

4. Replace the word in **bold** in this sentence with another word from the box which has a similar, but less formal, meaning (you will need to change the form of the word): "When he was caught stealing from the company, he was instantly **dismissed**".

5. Complete this sentence: The word *raise* in the box is similar in meaning to _____ (which is also in the box).

6. What is the difference between a *blue-collar worker* and a *white-collar worker*?

7. True or false?: When a company *downsizes* its work force, this means that it pays its workers less than before.

8. Complete this sentence: _____ are extra payments or benefits that you get in your job (for example, free meals, health insurance, company car, etc.).

9. What do you think *sick building syndrome* is?

10. Complete this sentence: If you have _____, you have work which is reliable and will last for a long time.

11. True or false?: *retire* and *resign* have the same meaning.

12. Complete this sentence: Banks, hospitals, and hotels are examples of _____.

13. Would you be happy if you had *adverse working conditions*?

14. Complete this sentence: A person who is _____ is not permanently employed by one company, but sells their services to more than one company.

Use your dictionary to check the meanings of the other words and expressions in the box.

Exercise 3
Complete this essay with appropriate words and expressions from the box in Exercise 1. You may need to change the form of some of the words.

"Some people live to work and others work to live. In most cases, this depends on the job they have and the conditions under which they are employed. In your opinion, what are the elements that make a job worthwhile?"

In answering this question, I would like to look first at the elements that combine to make a job undesirable. By avoiding such factors, potential (1) _____ are more likely to find a job that is more worthwhile, and by doing so, hope to achieve happiness in their work.

First of all, it doesn't matter if you are an (2) _____ worker cleaning the floor, a (3) _____ (4) _____ worker on a production line in one of the (5) _____, or a (6) _____ worker in a bank, store, or one of the other (7) _____: if you lack (8) _____, with the knowledge that you might lose your job at any time, you will never feel happy. Everybody would like a (9) _____ in which he or she is guaranteed work. Nowadays, however, companies have a high turnover of staff, (10) _____ new staff and (11) _____ others on a weekly basis. Such companies are not popular with their workers.

The same can be said of a job in which you are put under a lot of (12) _____ and worry, a job which is so (13) _____ that it takes over your life, a job where you work (14) _____ and so never get to see your family or friends, or a physical job in which you do the same thing every day and end up with the industrial disease that is always in the papers nowadays – (15) _____.

With all these negative factors, it would be difficult to believe that there are any elements that make a job worthwhile. Money is, of course, the prime motivator, and everybody wants a good (16) _____. But of course that is not all. The chance of (17) _____, of being given a better position in a company, is a motivating factor. Likewise, (18) _____ such as a free lunch or a company car, an (19) _____ plan to make you work hard such as a regular (20) _____ above the rate of inflation, (21) _____ in case you fall ill and a company (22) _____ plan so that you have some money when you retire all combine to make a job worthwhile.

Unfortunately, it is not always easy to find all of these. There is, however, an alternative. Forget the office and the factory floor and become (23) _____ and work for yourself. Your future may not be secure, but at least you will be happy.

Exercise 4
Now try this essay. Use words and expressions from the box in Exercise 1, and any other words or expressions that you think would be relevant.

"It is more important to have a job you enjoy doing than a job which pays well." How far do you agree with this statement? Use specific reasons and examples to support your answer.

Friends and relations

1. Use a dictionary to check the meanings of the words in the box. Can you think of any other words and expressions to add to the list?

acquaintance	admire	adore	amiable	(steady) boyfriend	be on good terms	best friend
bond	boss	bring up	brother	buddy	chemistry	classmate	be close to
cousin	coworker	crony	discipline	dysfunctional	empathize	empathy	encourage
encouragement	enemy	extended family	fall out with	family ties	fiancé / fiancée
be fond of	friendship	generous	get on with	(steady) girlfriend	grandparents
have a lot in common	husband	influence	in-laws	inseparable	inspire	inspiration
intimate	kind	kinship	love	nuclear family	nurture	parents	partner	raise
related	relative / relation	relationship	respect	room mate
see eye to eye	shared interests	siblings	sister	soul mate	spouse	supervisor	support
supportive	sympathize	sympathy	teacher	wife

2. Now try this essay. Use words and expressions from the box in Exercise 1, and any other words or expressions that you think would be relevant.

Different people influence our lives in different ways. How? Illustrate your answer with specific examples.

Global problems, social tensions, and solutions

1. Use a dictionary to check the meanings of the words in the box. Can you think of any other words and expressions to add to the list?

alien	charity	civil rights	cultural exchange program	culture	culture shock
differences	discriminate	discrimination	displaced people	emigrants
emigration	environment	equality	ethnic cleansing	exploit	exploitation	extremism
extremist	genocide	global village	homeless	homelessness	human rights	hunger
ignorance	illegal alien	immigrants	immigration	inequality
institutional racism	internally displaced	intolerance	language	migrants
nationalism	pollution	poverty	prejudice	racism	refugee	religion	religious
stateless people	study visit	terrorism	terrorist	tolerate
tolerance	UNESCO	UNHCR	UNICEF	xenophobia

2. Now try this essay. Use words and expressions from the box, and any other words or expressions that you think would be relevant.

The world today faces a lot of problems. Outline a few of these problems and suggest some things that ordinary people could do to make the world a better place.

Government and politics

1. Use a dictionary to check the meanings of the words in the box. Can you think of any other words and expressions to add to the list?

authoritarian   a bill   a candidate   to canvass   the Capitol   Capitol Hill   a committee   Congress   a congressman / congresswoman   a constituent assembly   a constitution   democratic   a democracy   a Democrat   to elect   an election   federal (law, tax, etc.)   freedom   a governor   the House of Representatives   ideology   independence   legislation   legislature   a monarchy   opposition   parliament   a politician   a president   a prime minister   to ratify   a referendum   represent   a republic   a Republican   sanctions   security   the Senate   a senator   a state   a statesman / stateswoman   a technocrat   totalitarian   to vote

2. Now try this essay. Use words and expressions from the box in Exercise 1, and any other words or expressions that you think would be relevant.

What, in your opinion, are most important things a government should do for its people? Support your answer with examples.

Health and exercise

1. Use a dictionary to check the meanings of the words in the box. Can you think of any other words and expressions to add to the list?

active   aerobics   balanced diet   cholesterol   cut down on (e.g., fatty foods, sugar)   disease   eating disorder   fall ill   fast food / junk food   fat   fibre   get fit   give up (e.g., smoking)   health club   heart attack   heart disease   in good shape   in poor shape   jogging   keep fit   lifestyle   look after (e.g., yourself, your health)   muscles   obese   obesity   on a diet   overweight   sedentary   skin problems   slim   sports center   swimming   take exercise   take up (e.g., a sport)   underweight   unhealthy

2. Now try this essay. Use words and expressions from the box, and any other words or expressions that you think would be relevant.

Too many young people these days are unhealthy and / or overweight. What advice would you give somebody who wanted to become fit and healthy?

Learning languages

1. Use a dictionary to check the meanings of the words in the box. Can you think of any other words and expressions to add to the list?

accent bilingual challenging communicate competent culture dictionary fluent	

accent   bilingual   challenging   communicate   competent   culture   dictionary   fluent
get by (in a language)   grammar   learn something parrot fashion   lingua franca
look up (in a dictionary)   monolingual   mother tongue   multilingual   native
pick up (a language)   practice   progress   pronunciation   rewarding
second language   self-access centre   vocabulary

2. Now try this essay. Use words and expressions from the box in Exercise 1, and any other words or expressions that you think would be relevant.

What are the most effective ways of learning a foreign language? Illustrate your answer with specific examples.

Movies and the theater

1. Use a dictionary to check the meanings of the words in the box. Can you think of any other words and expressions to add to the list?

acting   action   actor / actress   animation   atmosphere   audience   believable   big budget
box office   cartoon   cast   climax   comedy   director   documentary   drama
entertaining   exciting   feel-good   funny   gritty   horror   location   movie   musical
performance   plot   romance   scenery   science fiction   screen   setting   soundtrack
special effects   stars   story   thriller   video

2. Now try this essay. Use words and expressions from the box, and any other words or expressions that you think would be relevant.

What kinds of movies do you enjoy watching, and why do you enjoy watching them? Use specific examples to explain your answer.

Music

1. Use a dictionary to check the meanings of the words in the box. Can you think of any other words and expressions to add to the list?

aggressive   an album   an artist(e)   beat   blues (music)   a classic   classical music   a compilation   to compose   a composer   a concert   to conduct   a conductor   contemporary   dance music   download   easy listening   heavy metal   a hit   improvise   improvisation   innovative   jazz   live (adjective)   lively   lyrics   mellow   memorable   mood   opera   orchestra   percussion   pop   popular   rap   to record   recorded   reggae   relaxing   rock music   sentimental   a singer-songwriter   a soloist   strings   vocalist   vocals   wind instrument   world music

2. Now try this essay. Use words and expressions from the box in Exercise 1, and any other words or expressions that you think would be relevant.

The music you listen to says a lot about the kind of person you are. How far do you agree with this? Use specific reasons and examples to support your answer.

Sports

1. Use a dictionary to check the meanings of the words in the box. Can you think of any other words and expressions to add to the list?

arena   athlete   athletics   beat   coach   competitive   competitor   course   court   draw   equalize   exercise   go (swimming, jogging, climbing, etc.)   hooligan   hooliganism   lose   match   opponent   opposition   pitch   play (baseball, tennis, basketball, etc.)   prize   referee   score   spectator   spectator sports   sponsor   sponsorship   sportsman / sportswoman   stadium   support   supporter   take up (a sport)   team   team spirit   team sports   train   trainer   umpire   unite   violence   win

2. Now try this essay. Use words and expressions from the box, and any other words or expressions that you think would be relevant.

Do you agree or disagree with the following statement? Sports play an important role in a culture. Use specific reasons and examples to support your answer.

Your hometown

1. Use a dictionary to check the meanings of the words in the box. Can you think of any other words and expressions to add to the list?

amenities busy character college community community spirit congestion crime demolish (old buildings) eating out environment healthcare historic homeless homelessness hospital housing housing project improve improvement increase industry job opportunities library livelihood lively local customs mall modern monument museum neighbor neighborhood nightlife noise control park peaceful pedestrianize pollution population preserve (old buildings) reduce rejuvenate renovate restaurants rural safe shopping sports center sports facilities statue street crime theater traditional traffic traffic calming traffic-free urban zoo

2. Now try this essay. Use words and expressions from the box in Exercise 1, and any other words or expressions that you think would be relevant.

You have been asked for some suggestions to make your hometown a better place. What suggestions would you make, and why?

Vocabulary record sheet

Photocopy this page as many times as you like, and use it to keep a record of new words and expressions that you learn. Try to build up your own vocabulary bank, and keep this in a file or folder with the words / expressions stored in alphabetical order for quick and easy reference. Review the items that you have recorded on a regular basis. See the next page for a model record sheet showing an example of how a vocabulary item has been recorded.

Word or expression:	
Topic area(s) (if relevant):	
Definition(s):	
Translation or equivalent in my language:	
Other forms of this word (if relevant):	
Sample sentences:	
Other collocations:	
Related words and expressions:	
Other information:	

You may photocopy this page

Vocabulary record sheet sample

This is a sample of a completed vocabulary sheet, based on the word "reject". The student has included as much information about the word as possible, including its grammatical function and pronunciation.

Word or expression:	reject (verb, regular, transitive) / rɪ'dʒekt /
Topic area(s) (if relevant):	Accepting or refusing something
Definition(s):	1. to not agree to an offer, proposal or request. 2. to disagree with an idea, argument or suggestion. 3. To refuse to take something, maybe because it is damaged. 4. to behave in an unkind way to someone who wants kindness or love. 5. (of a human body) to reject an organ after a transplant.
Translation or equivalent in my language:	rejeter / refuser
Other forms of this word (if relevant):	reject, rejection (noun)
Sample sentences:	It is almost certain that our offer will be rejected. The court rejected the defendant's argument. The company rejected the whole shipment. He claimed he had been rejected by his parents. His body rejected the new kidney and he became seriously ill.
Other collocations:	to reject categorically / decisively / firmly / flatly / outright / totally / unanimously / vigorously. With the exception of "outright", these adverbs can also come <u>before</u> the word "reject".
Related words and expressions:	refuse, decline, turn down, throw out, veto, dismiss, rebuff, shun, snub, take a rain check (idiom) ("Would you like to come out tonight?" "I'll take a rain check, if that's OK with you")

Other information:

The opposite of reject is <u>accept</u>. The opposite of rejection is <u>acceptance</u>.

Reject is often used with as + an adjective or adjective phrase:

"He rejected the idea as ridiculous". "She rejected my offer as being too expensive".

If we reject something completely, we can say that we reject it "out of hand".

Answer key

Addition, equation, and conclusion (page 4)

Exercise 1

Addition:	and along with as well as also too in addition besides what's more furthermore moreover along with (this could also be equation)
Equation:	equally likewise similarly in the same way correspondingly along with (this could also be addition)
Conclusion:	in conclusion to sum up briefly it can be concluded that to conclude in brief thus to summarize therefore

Exercise 2

1. Furthermore / Moreover / In addition / What's more (this is less formal than the other expressions)   **2.** As well as / Besides
3. Likewise / Similarly / In the same way (the verbs in both sentences – i.e., *respect* – are the same and refer to the same thing, so we can use a word of equation here)   **4.** As well as / Along with   **5.** In addition   **6.** Likewise / Similarly   **7.** Likewise / In the same way / Correspondingly   **8.** In brief   **9.** It can be concluded that   **10.** Therefore (*To sum up, To conclude* and *To summarize* are usually used to conclude longer pieces of writing – e.g., at the end of an essay. *Thus* is slightly more formal than therefore, but has the same meaning)

Note: It is important that you are familiar with the way these words and expressions are used, including the other words in a sentence that they "work" with. Use a dictionary to look up examples of these words and expressions, and keep a record of them to refer to the next time you use them.

"American" English (pages 5 –7)

Across

2. intermission   **6.** over (in the context of repeating something completely only. In other contexts, *again* is used in the same way as it is used in British English)   **8.** mail   **9.** recognize (note that in British English, this word can be spelt *recognise* or *recognize*)*   **11.** theater*   **13.** underpass   **16.** gas   **18.** elevator   **20.** realtors   **24.** highway   **26.** raise   **27.** recess   **29.** guy   **30.** faculty**   **32.** fall   **35.** sedan   **36.** store   **37.** defense*   **38.** round-trip   **40.** alumnus   **41.** cellphone

Down

1. zip code   **3.** through   **4.** movies (*movie theater* is also used)   **5.** bill   **7.** labor*   **10.** gotten   **12.** apartments   **14.** travelers*   **15.** first   **17.** sidewalk   **19.** movie   **21.** freeway (*expressway* is also used)   **22.** this   **23.** dialog*   **25.** drugstore   **28.** subway   **31.** attorney (*lawyer* is also used)   **33.** eraser   **34.** vacation   **39.** bathroom

* Note the following spelling differences between British and American English:

• Words which usually end in *-ise* in British English end with *-ize* in American English (*recognize, realize, itemize*, etc.)
• Words which end with *-re* in British English usually end with *-er* in American English (*theater, center, liter*, etc.)
• Words which end with *-our* in British English normally end with *-or* in American English (*humor, labor, color*, etc.)
• Words which end with *-ogue* in British English normally end with just *-og* in American English (*dialog, catalog*, etc.)
• Words which end in *-ence* in British English end with *-ense* in American English (*pretense, defense, offense*, etc.)
• Words which end with *-amme* in British English usually just end with *-am* in American English (*kilogram, program, telegram*, etc.)
• Words with a double *L* in the middle in British English (such as *traveller* or *travelling*) usually use a single *L* in American English (*traveler, traveling*, etc.), but some words that use a single *L* followed by a consonant in British English use a double *L* in American English (*skillful, installment*).

There are other spelling differences which do not follow any particular "rules", and these words have to be learned individually (for example, *judgement* in British English can be spelled the same way in American English, but many North Americans also spell it *judgment*). Also see the note on *practice* in the answer key for *Spelling* Exercise 2 on page 120).

** This is one of several words which are used in both British and American English, but which have a different meaning (often depending on the context in which they are used). In this case, *faculty* is usually used by North Americans to talk about the people who work in a school, college, university, etc., while in British English it is used to talk about a particular department in a university (e.g., *the Humanities Faculty*). *Gas* (see 16 across) in American English is a short form of *gasoline*. The word *gasoline* is also used in British English, but the word *petrol* is more common: British-English speakers normally use the word *gas* to talk about a substance that is used to heat the house or cook food. To make things more complicated, it also has the same meaning in North America.

Changes (pages 8 – 9)

Exercise 1

1. True   **2.** True   **3.** False: there has been an *improvement*   **4.** False: there has been an *increase*   **5.** False: there has been a *strengthening* of the dollar   **6.** False: there has been a *relaxation* of border controls   **7.** False: we're *increasing* or *building up* our stock of coal   **8.** True   **9.** False: there has been a *slight* fall   **10.** False: they're going to *decrease* the number   **11.** False: there has been a *decline*   **12.** False: there has been a *tightening up* of the rules   **13.** False: there has been a *widening* of the gap   **14.** True   **15.** False: there has been a *downward* trend   **16.** True   **17.** True   **18.** True   **19.** True   **20.** False: Americans want to *broaden* their horizons.

Most of the words in this task can be verbs as well as nouns. Use a dictionary to check which ones.

Exercise 2

The words in the box are:
adapt replace expand promote reduce transform switch renovate exchange demote alter disappear vary raise lower extend enlarge heighten lengthen deepen shorten stretch revise amend cut outsource deteriorate streamline upgrade restructure downsize

1. exchanged   **2.** adapt   **3.** transformed   **4.** renovated   **5.** switch   **6.** vary   **7.** expands   **8.** deteriorating   **9.** revised *or* amended (*revised* prices are usually increased, but they can also go down, as in this example. This verb in this context is usually used in the passive voice)   **10.** stretched

Comparing and contrasting (page 10)

1. contrast   **2.** differ   **3.** differentiate   **4.** characteristics   **5.** distinction   **6.** Compared   **7.** comparison   **8.** similar to   **9.** similarities   **10.** In the same way   **11.** Likewise   **12.** By way of contrast   **13.** Nevertheless / Even so / However (*Even so* is more common in spoken than in written English)   **14.** discrepancy   **15.** whereas

Condition and requirement (page 11)

1. As long as   **2.** Unless   **3.** on condition that (*that* = optional)   **4.** providing that (*that* = optional. We can also say *provided that*)   **5.** preconditions   **6.** In case of (note that in this particular expression, we do not say *In case of a fire*. In other situations, an article or pronoun would be needed after *in case of*)   **7.** in the event of   **8.** stipulation   **9.** unconditional   **10.** Assuming that (*that* = optional)   **11.** on the assumption that (*that* = optional)   **12.** prerequisites   **13.** terms / conditions   **14.** requirement   **15.** Failing that (*that* is needed here, as it refers back to the previous sentence. *Failing that* means that if the first option – *telephoning us* – is not possible, you should try the second option – *send us an email*)   **16.** otherwise

Confusing words and false friends (pages 12 – 14)

1. action / activity   **2.** advise / advice   **3.** effect / affect   **4.** appreciable / appreciative   **5.** assumption / presumption   **6.** prevent / avoid   **7.** beside / besides   **8.** shortly / briefly   **9.** channel / canal   **10.** conscious / conscientious   **11.** continuous / continual   **12.** inspect / control   **13.** objections / criticism   **14.** injury / damage / harm   **15.** invent / discover   **16.** for / during / while   **17.** However / Moreover   **18.** considerable / considerate   **19.** intolerable / intolerant   **20.** job / work   **21.** lies / lay   **22.** watch / look at   **23.** permit / permission   **24.** possibility / chance   **25.** priceless / worthless   **26.** principle / principal / principal / principle   **27.** procession / process   **28.** rise / raise   **29.** respectful / respectable   **30.** treat / cure   **31.** subjective / objective   **32.** disinterested / uninterested or disinterested (it is a common misconception in English that *disinterested* cannot be used in the same way as *uninterested* when we want to say that someone does not find something interesting)   **33.** infer / imply   **34.** complementary / complimentary

Answer key

Idioms and colloquialisms 1 (pages 15 – 16)

Here are the most suitable answers:

<u>Exercise 1</u>
1. I really don't mind. It's up to you.   **2.** You've got to be kidding!   **3.** I couldn't agree more.   **4.** No way! Not a chance! *or* You've got to be kidding!   **5.** Let me sleep on it.   **6.** It does nothing for me.   **7.** You really should get a life or You've got to be kidding!   **8.** I couldn't care less.   **9.** Wow! Way to go!   **10.** Why not? Go for it!   **11.** You're welcome, but it was nothing really.   **12.** Never mind. It can't be helped.

<u>Exercise 2</u>
1. Sure. Why not? *or* You bet!   **2.** How's it going?   **3.** How should I know?   **4.** What a drag!   **5.** You bet!   **6.** I'm going to give it all I've got.   **7.** Oh, I'm used to it.   **8.** What do you have in mind?   **9.** You're out of luck.   **10.** Let me lend a hand.   **11.** I'm a bit tied up for the time being.   **12.** Is it any wonder?

Idioms and colloquialisms 2 (pages 17 – 18)

<u>Exercise 1</u>
1. I'd be glad to (this is a polite way of agreeing to do something).   **2.** Be my guest (this is a polite way of giving somebody permission to do something).   **3.** A little bird told me (we say this when we don't want to say who said something to us).   **4.** My lips are sealed (we say this when we promise to keep a secret, or when we refuse to tell someone a secret).   **5.** I'm keeping my fingers crossed (we say this when we are hoping that something will happen).   **6.** Rather you than me (this means that we are glad we are not doing something that somebody else is).   **7.** Fire away, I'm all ears (this means that we are ready to listen to something).   **8.** Now you're talking (we say this when somebody suggests something that is more acceptable or enjoyable than something else they have already suggested).   **9.** I'm having second thoughts (this means that we will probably change our mind about something we have already agreed to).   **10.** That'll be the day (this means that we don't believe something will happen. We can also say "And pigs might fly!" or "I'll believe it when I see it")   **11.** Who let the cat out of the bag? (we say this when we want to know who revealed something that was supposed to be a secret, a surprise, etc.)   **12.** That'll teach you! (this means that the person who is complaining has only themselves to blame)

<u>Exercise 2</u>
1. Oh, this is on me (we say this when we are offering to pay for something).   **2.** Congratulations (this is another way of saying "Well done").   **3.** I'd love to (we say this when we are accepting an offer to do something)   **4.** You're welcome (this is another way of saying "Not at all" or "Don't mention it").   **5.** Thanks. Make yourself at home (this is an expression we use when somebody visits our house).   **6.** Hold on (an informal expression which means "Wait").   **7.** Yes. Take care and keep in touch (an expression we use when we will not see somebody for a while).   **8.** Couldn't be better (this means that we are very well).   **9.** I'd rather you didn't (this is a polite way of telling somebody that you don't want them to do something).   **10.** Oh, that's too bad (this is another way of saying "Hard luck", "Bad luck", or "Tough luck", and we use it to sympathize with someone)   **11.** The name doesn't ring any bells (this means that you do not recognize the name)   **12.** Sure, touch wood ("Touch wood" is an expression we use when we hope that something will, or won't, happen)

<u>Exercise 3</u>
1. How's it going? (an informal way of asking somebody if something is going well or badly)   **2.** I'll say (when we agree completely with somebody)   **3.** Not on your life! (an informal way of saying that we would never do something)   **4.** That's a load off my mind. (when we are suddenly no longer worried about something that was troubling us. We can also say "That's a weight off my mind")   **5.** Well, keep it to yourself (= don't tell anyone else, usually because something is, or should be, a secret)   **6.** Sure thing (an informal way of saying we agree to do something)   **7.** Of course, take a seat ("Take a seat" means "Sit down")   **8.** Well, take it easy. Don't kill yourself. (these are informal ways of telling somebody not to work too hard, or to calm down, relax)   **9.** Oh well, it's not the end of the world (this means that things are probably not as bad as they seem).   **10.** Have a good time (we want the person to whom we are speaking to enjoy themselves)   **11.** So I guess you're in the doghouse again (if you are "in the doghouse", you are in trouble with someone)   **12.** Gesundheit! (this is something we say when someone sneezes. We can also say "Bless you!")

Idioms and colloquialisms 3 (pages 19 – 20)

1. U   **2.** S   **3.** T   **4.** F   **5.** X   **6.** A   **7.** C   **8.** H   **9.** P   **10.** Q   **11.** W   **12.** G   **13.** R   **14.** L   **15.** O   **16.** V   **17.** K   **18.** I   **19.** E   **20.** J   **21.** N   **22.** D   **23.** Z   **24.** Y   **25.** M   **26.** B

Answer key

Idioms and colloquialisms 4 (pages 21 – 22)

Exercise 1
1. candle **2.** worms **3.** bull **4.** nose **5.** blind **6.** track **7.** pressed **8.** weather **9.** blue **10.** question **11.** record **12.** ground **13.** ice **14.** air **15.** shop **16.** ground **17.** close **18.** picture

Exercise 2
1. name **2.** world **3.** strings **4.** played **5.** red **6.** good **7.** out **8.** ground **9.** level **10.** can **11.** flow **12.** parade **13.** leaf **14.** break **15.** running **16.** large **17.** five **18.** sixth

Metaphors (pages 23 – 25)

Exercise 1
1. edifice **2.** sow the seeds **3.** constructed **4.** buttressed **5.** deep-rooted **6.** architect **7.** laid the foundations **8.** towering or ground-breaking **9.** blueprint **10.** build up **11.** build on **12.** under construction **13.** collapsed **14.** ground-breaking **15.** ruins **16.** demolished **17.** fertile **18.** took root **19.** stemmed from **20.** fruitful

Exercise 2
(These are suggested answers, and you might choose other words which are equally suitable)
1. argument **2.** intelligence **3.** assist **4.** important / unimportant **5.** effort **6.** knowledge **7.** opportunity **8.** discover **9.** life *or* career **10.** force **11.** intelligence **12.** conversation / discussion **13.** problem **14.** enthusiasm / excitement **15.** successful / failure

The *Macmillan English Dictionary for Advanced Learners*, from which many of the definitions and sample sentences in this exercise have been taken, has very useful sections on metaphors under the following entries:

achieve, afraid, aim, angry, argument, busy, communicate, confused, conversation, criticize, deceive, difficulty, discover, effort, enthusiasm, feeling, force, friendly, guilty, happy, hate, help, honest, idea, illness, important, intelligence, interested, knowledge, language, life, love, method, mind, mistake, money, nervous, opinion, opportunity, organization, people, power, problem, proud, quantity, relationship, responsibility, search, secret, self, sensible, simple, situation, strange, success, time, tolerance, understand, want, win.

Make a note of those that you think are the most useful, and try to use them in your English. Note that the words and expressions that come towards the end of each metaphor box are more informal and idiomatic than those at the beginning, and would normally only be used in more informal spoken situations.

Numbers and symbols (page 26)

1. 2006 = two thousand (and) six (some people also say *twenty oh six*) / 1994 = nineteen ninety four **2.** 24/7 = twenty four seven (= 24 hours a day, 7 days a week) **3.** 0.8% = zero point eight percent **4.** 3:45 = three forty five, or quarter of four* **5.** 1800 = eighteen hundred (hours) **6.** June 30 = the thirtieth of June or June thirtieth **7.** 10/3 = the third of October / October third (in the USA) or the tenth of March / March the tenth (in the UK). Alternatively, you could say *the third of the tenth* **8.** 27½ = twenty seven and a half **9.** ¾ = three quarters or three fourths **10.** 6ft. x 3ft. x 3ft. = six feet by three feet by three feet** **11.** $1.99 = one dollar ninety nine (or *one dollar and ninety nine cents*) **12.** $100.99 = one hundred dollars ninety nine (or *one hundred dollars and ninety nine cents*) **13.** $120.75 = one hundred twenty dollars seventy five (or *one hundred twenty dollars and seventy five cents*) / $1120.75 = One thousand, one hundred twenty dollars seventy five (or *one thousand, one hundred twenty dollars and seventy five cents*) **14.** ACB81 - 25/B = ACB eighty one dash (or *hyphen*) 25 slash (or *stroke*) B **15.** (212) 909-7940 = two one two, nine oh nine, seven nine four oh *or* area code two one two, nine oh nine, seven nine four oh **16.** 1-800-528-4800 = one eight hundred, five two eight, four eight oh oh **17.** 1-800-AXP-1234 = one eight hundred, A X P, one two three four **18.** 999 = nine nine nine / 911 = nine one one / 000 = triple oh **19.** # = pound / 0 = zero / * = star **20.** $200K = two hundred thousand dollars / mid-50's = mid-fifties **21.** $6M = six million dollars **22.** 2:1 = two to one (when talking about odds and ratios) **23.** @snailmail.com = at Snailmail dot com **24.** GR8 = great / :-) = happy / CUL8R = see you later (informal abbreviations and emoticons*** such as these are commonly used in text messages, notes, and email) **25.** 4x4 = four by four (a vehicle with four-wheel drive, also called a *4WD* or *SUV – Sports Utility Vehicle*) **26.** 2:0 = two zero / 3:3 = three all **27.** 37,762,418 = thirty seven million, seven hundred sixty two thousand, four hundred eighteen **28.** 1099 = ten ninety nine (this is a document that people in the USA send to the IRS – the US tax department – that gives details of the money they have earned during the year other than their salary) **29.** © = copyright (the material cannot be copied without permission) **30.** ® = registered (the name is registered, and cannot be used by another company for another product)

* In British English, people say *(a) quarter <u>to</u> four*. Note that for times before the half hour, people say *past* in British English

Answer key

and *after* in American English (for example, 4.10 is ten *past* four in British English, and ten *after* four in American English).

** A foot is a unit of measurement used in the U.K. and the U.S.A. which is equal to about 30cm. A foot is divided into 12 inches.

*** **:-)** is an *emoticon*, a symbol that shows emotion. Emoticons take the form of a face on its side, and use standard punctuation symbols and letters. In this case, it is a smiling face to show happiness. Other emoticons include **:-(** to show unhappiness, **:-0** to show surprise, **:-||** to show anger, **:-@** to show fear, **:-X** to indicate a kiss. Some computers automatically turn some emoticons into proper faces (for example, by entering **:-)**, the computer automatically makes a ☺).

Obligation and option (page 27)

1. required (not *mandatory* or *compulsory*, as these cannot be followed with *by*)   **2.** compulsory   **3.** must (not *have*, as this must be followed with *to*)   **4.** have / need   **5.** liable (not *obliged* or *compelled*, as these must be followed with *to*)   **6.** forced (this is better than *obliged* or *compelled*, as it is stronger and suggests that the company has no other choice. Also, *obliged* and *compelled* are usually used when somebody makes somebody else do something)   **7.** exempt   **8.** Mandatory (this is better than *Compulsory*, as it suggests the checks must be carried out because of a law: see 2 above)   **9.** voluntary (not *optional*, as the gap is preceded by *a*, not *an*)   **10.** optional (not *voluntary*, as the gap is preceded by *an*)   **11.** alternative (used as part of an expression: "*We have no alternative but to…*")   **12.** obliged / required   **13.** obligation (note the adjective form of obliged / obligation = *obligatory*)   **14.** compelled (in other words, he felt that people were putting pressure on him to make him leave. We could also use *obliged*)   **15.** entail (we can also say *involve*)   **16.** need (used here as a noun)   **17.** essential (*vital* or *imperative* could also be used)

Opinion, attitude and belief (pages 28 – 30)

Exercise 1
1. concerned   **2.** opinion   **3.** maintains   **4.** suspect   **5.** exception   **6.** regarding   **7.** convinced   **8.** fanatical (the noun is *fanatic*)   **9.** doubt   **10.** traditional   **11.** disapprove   **12.** committed   **13.** conservative

Exercise 2
1. intellectual (this can also be an adjective)   **2.** royalist (this can also be an adjective)   **3.** socialism (*socialist* is the adjective and also the word for someone who supports this system)   **4.** capitalism (*capitalist* is the adjective and also the word for someone who supports this system adjective and also the word for someone who supports this system)   **5.** communism (*communist* is the adjective and also the word for someone who supports this system)   **6.** vegan (vegans practice *veganism*)   **7.** vegetarian (vegetarians practice *vegetarianism*)   **8.** obsessive   **9.** middle-of-the-road   **10.** tolerant   **11.** moral   **12.** racist (This can also be an adjective. *Racism* is the name for this attitude)   **13.** open-minded   **14.** dogmatic   **15.** anarchist (*anarchy* is the name for this belief)   **16.** stoical (a person who is stoical is a *stoic*)   **17.** bigoted (a person who is bigoted is a *bigot*)   **18.** pragmatic (a person who is pragmatic is a *pragmatist*)   **19.** moderate (this can also be an adjective)   **20.** opinionated   **21.** Republican (the second definition uses a lower-case *r*: *republican*)   **22.** Democrat (the second definition uses a lower-case *d*: *democrat*. The political system is a *democracy*. The adjective is *democratic*)   **23.** Islam (the adjective is *Islamic*)   **24.** Muslim (this can also be an adjective)   **25.** Christianity   **26.** Christian (this can also be an adjective)   **27.** Judaism   **28.** Jew (the adjective is *Jewish*)   **29.** Hinduism   **30.** Hindu (this can also be an adjective)   **31.** Sikhism (a follower of this religion is a *Sikh*)   **32.** Buddhism (a follower of this religion is a *Buddhist*)   **33.** Taoism (a follower of this belief is a *Taoist*)   **34.** egalitarian   **35.** fascism (someone who believes in fascism is a *fascist*)   **36.** atheist (*atheistic* is the adjective. *Atheism* is the name of this belief)   **37.** agnostic (This can also be an adjective. *Agnosticism* is the name of this belief)   **38.** cynic (the adjective is *cynical*)   **39.** pacifist   **40.** superstitious

Opposites 1: Verbs (pages 31 – 33)

Exercise 1
1. rejected   **2.** denied   **3.** refused   **4.** attacked   **5.** demolished   **6.** simplified   **7.** abandoned   **8.** withdrew   **9.** deteriorated   **10.** forbade   **11.** rewarded   **12.** lowered   **13.** set   **14.** fell   **15.** loosened   **16.** succeeded   **17.** postponed   **18.** lend   **19.** concealed   **20.** extended   **21.** exaggerate   **22.** declined   **23.** replenished   **24.** gained   **25.** abolished   **26.** hired

Exercise 2
Across **2.** misquoted   **3.** misdiagnosing   **6.** discontinuing   **8.** misrepresent   **10.** unloaded   **12.** disagree   **13.** misuses   **14.** unlock   **16.** unfolded   **20.** distrust *or* mistrust   **22.** disapproved   **23.** disobeyed
Down **1.** misjudged   **2.** misunderstands   **4.** disconnecting   **5.** disqualified   **7.** displeased   **9.** miscalculated   **11.** misbehave   **15.** disallowed   **17.** misplaced   **18.** uncovered (*not* discovered)   **19.** disproved   **21.** dislike

Opposites 2: Adjectives (pages 34 – 35)

Exercise 1
1. clear **2.** easy **3.** graceful **4.** detrimental **5.** approximate **6.** innocent **7.** even **8.** scarce **9.** flexible
10. considerable **11.** crude **12.** delicate **13.** dim **14.** compulsory **15.** reluctant **16.** archaic **17.** worthwhile
18. vibrant **19.** tedious **20.** spontaneous **21.** intricate **22.** worthless **23.** negligible **24.** feasible **25.** commonplace
26. problematic **27.** smooth **28.** artificial

Exercise 2
Task 1
unacceptable   inaccurate   inadequate   disadvantaged   disagreeable   unattractive   unauthorized   unavoidable
unbelievable   uncertain   uncomfortable   incompetent   incomplete   unconscious   discontented   unconvincing
incorrect   incurable   uneven   unfair   unfashionable   dishonest   disinclined   illegal   unlimited   illiterate   illogical
unmarried   immature   immoral   immortal   disobedient   disorganized   impatient   imperfect   impersonal   impossible
improper   impure   unqualified (*disqualified* is a verb which means to make someone not able to do something: "*He was
disqualified from driving for a year*")   irrational   irregular   irrelevant   irreplaceable   irresistible   irresolute   irresponsible
unsatisfactory   dissatisfied   insufficient   unwelcome

Note that adjectives which end with *-ful* are usually made into their opposite form by changing *-ful* to *-less* (*thoughtful* =
thoughtless, *useful* = *useless*, etc.). *Helpful* is one exception to this rule (the opposite is *unhelpful*. *Helpless* has a different
meaning, and means *not able to do anything*)

Task 2
1. D (= disinclined) **2.** B (= dishonest) **3.** C (= insufficient) **4.** A (= irresponsible) **5.** C (= unconvincing) **6.** A (=
inadequate)

Phrasal verbs 1 (pages 36 – 37)

Exercise 1
1. bring up **2.** face up to **3.** call off **4.** count on **5.** catch up with **6.** die down **7.** drop out of **8.** figure out
9. fell out **10.** find out **11.** grow up **12.** keep up with **13.** leaves out **14.** pointed out **15.** look into **16.** brought
up **17.** fall behind **18.** cut down on

Exercise 2
1. taken over **2.** put forward **3.** pull through **4.** done away with **5.** look into **6.** carry out **7.** went, kept, or carried
on **8.** wear off **9.** turn up **10.** picked up **11.** put across **12.** ran into **13.** set…back **14.** look back on
15. turned out **16.** turned away **17.** works out to **18.** cut off

Phrasal verbs 2 (pages 38 – 39)
Exercise 1
1. get **2.** look *or* go **3.** get **4.** get *or* come **5.** look **6.** go **7.** get **8.** went **9.** look **10.** look **11.** came **12.**
look **13.** get **14.** give **15.** came **16.** go **17.** get **18.** go

Exercise 2
1. came *or* went **2.** give **3.** go *or* look **4.** get **5.** came **6.** get **7.** give **8.** go **9.** come *or* go **10.** came **11.**
come **12.** getting **13.** comes **14.** get **15.** give **16.** look **17.** give **18.** got

Phrasal verbs 3 (pages 40 – 42)

Across:
1. put down **5.** talk…around **6.** take after **7.** running up against **9.** turn out **10.** picked on **11.** opt out
16. turned up **19.** set off **20.** run up **22.** set aside (or *put aside*) **24.** take to **28.** take up **30.** held up **32.** engaged
in **36.** set off **37.** factoring in **38.** running out **39.** handing in

Down:
1. put aside (*set aside* – see 22 across – has the same meaning, but would not work in the crossword grid) **2.** take in
3. add up to **4.** taken in **6.** turned down **8.** put up with **12.** taken apart **13.** set…against **14.** make out
15. made up **17.** ran for **18.** pick up **21.** make up for **23.** set up **25.** kick in **26.** stemmed from **27.** pull out
29. shut out of **31.** bring about **33.** gone down with **34.** break into **35.** went for

Answer key

Prefixes (pages 43 – 44)

<u>Exercise 1</u>
1. (k)   **2.** (i)   **3.** (j)   **4.** (e)   **5.** (b)   **6.** (l)   **7.** (f)   **8.** (a)   **9.** (g)   **10.** (c)   **11.** (h)   **12.** m   **13.** (d)   **14.** (f)

<u>Exercise 2</u>
1. postgraduate   **2.** monotonous   **3.** uniform   **4.** translate   **5.** semifinal (sometimes written as two words: *semi final*)
6. intermission *or* interval   **7.** cohesion   **8.** teleconference   **9.** biannual   **10.** biennial   **11.** circumference
12. autobiography   **13.** postpone   **14.** circumvent   **15.** microscope   **16.** unique   **17.** premature   **18.** substandard
19. cohabit   **20.** microorganism (sometimes written as two words: *micro organism*)   **21.** transmutes   **22.** monopoly
23. predetermined   **24.** bilingual   **25.** autonomy   **26.** transient   **27.** subordinate   **28.** semi-precious (note that some
words which are modified by *semi* are hyphenated: *semi-skilled*, *semi-permanent*, *semi-conscious*, etc.)

Note: Rather confusingly, a *biweekly* magazine can either be a magazine that is published once every two weeks, *or* twice
a week. This also applies to publications which are *bimonthly*. To avoid confusion, we can say that magazines that are
published twice a week or twice a month are *semi-weekly* or *semi-monthly*.

Presenting an argument (page 45)

<u>Exercise 1</u>
The best order is: **1.** A   **2.** H   **3.** K   **4.** M   **5.** E   **6.** G   **7.** B   **8.** J   **9.** F   **10.** O   **11.** L   **12.** N   **13.** L   **14.** D   **15.** I
16. P

When you are asked to present an argument (e.g., in an essay), you should always look at it from two sides, giving reasons
why you agree and disagree before reaching a conclusion. It is usually best to present your strongest argument in favor of
something just before you write the conclusion.

Other words and expressions which you might find useful include:
I believe that   despite this   in spite of this   also   thirdly   I think   finally   in conclusion   nonetheless   admittedly
on the contrary   at any rate   notwithstanding   for all that   even if

Pronouns and determiners (pages 46 – 47)

<u>Exercise 1</u>
1. there   **2.** their   **3.** it   **4.** them (used when we do not specify if the caller was male or female)   **5.** himself   **6.** they
7. that   **8.** which   **9.** it   **10.** their   **11.** its (do not confuse the possessive *its* with *it's*, which is a contraction of *it is* or *it
has*)   **12.** There   **13.** that   **14.** them   **15.** which   **16.** itself   **17.** it   **18.** they   **19.** those   **20.** itself

<u>Exercise 2</u>
1. that or which (alternatively, you could leave the space blank. *That* or *which*, when used as pronouns in defining relative
clauses such as this, can be left out when they are the object of the relative clause)   **2.** whose   **3.** there   **4.** themselves
5. which   **6.** those   **7.** their   **8.** that   **9.** which   **10.** those   **11.** them   **12.** its   **13.** theirs   **14.** they   **15.** whose
16. that *or* which (or leave this space blank – see number 1 above)   **17.** ourselves   **18.** itself   **19.** them   **20.** themselves

Similar meanings: Adjectives 1 (pages 48 – 49)

1. abrupt   **2.** robust   **3.** rudimentary   **4.** nominal   **5.** conventional   **6.** curious   **7.** expert   **8.** remote   **9.** absurd
10. compatible   **11.** legitimate   **12.** rigid   **13.** placid   **14.** narrow   **15.** covert   **16.** negligible   **17.** hazardous
18. contemporary   **19.** enduring   **20.** exceptional   **21.** outlandish   **22.** prompt   **23.** outdated   **24.** prospective
25. comprehensive   **26.** adequate   **27.** steady   **28.** dramatic   **29.** thriving   **30.** complex   **31.** inventive   **32.** potent
33. radical   **34.** shallow   **35.** erratic   **36.** fertile   **37.** even   **38.** crucial / indispensable   **39.** varied.   **40.** crucial /
indispensable   **41.** toxic   **42.** incisive   **43.** finite   **44.** widespread   **45.** resolute   **46.** coarse

Similar meanings: Adjectives 2 (page 50)

1. concise   **2.** handsome   **3.** archaic   **4.** risky   **5.** abundant   **6.** chaotic   **7.** tedious   **8.** evident   **9.** rampant
10. integral   **11.** scrupulous   **12.** tenacious   **13.** industrious   **14.** credible

The word in the shaded vertical strip is *characteristic*.

Similar meanings: Nouns (pages 51 – 53)

Exercise 1
1. agenda / schedule   **2.** accommodations / housing   **3.** discipline / order   **4.** assistance / help   **5.** drop / decline
6. faults / defects   **7.** opposition / resistance   **8.** proof / evidence   **9.** discount / reduction   **10.** proximity / closeness
11. appointment / meeting   **12.** acclaim / praise   **13.** work / employment   **14.** benefits / advantages   **15.** requirements
/ prerequisites   **16.** means (note that in this context, means is always used in the plural) / method   **17.** poll / survey
18. victory / triumph   **19.** fallacy / misconception   **20.** appeal / petition

Exercise 2
1. protest / demonstration   **2.** code / rules   **3.** liability / responsibility   **4.** choices / options   **5.** overview / (short)
description   **6.** magnitude / importance   **7.** cooperation / collaboration   **8.** valid / good   **9.** zenith / peak   **10.** questions
/ queries   **11.** characteristics / features (with illnesses, we can also say *symptoms*)   **12.** problems / complications
13. strategy / plan   **14.** priority / precedence   **15.** alterations / changes   **16.** winner / victor   **17.** component / element
18. discussion / deliberation   **19.** results / consequences   **20.** admission / access

Exercise 3
1. reviews / write-ups   **2.** advent / appearance   **3.** charisma / (personal) appeal   **4.** category / classification   **5.** ending /
termination   **6.** inventions (or *achievements*) / innovations   **7.** numbers / concentrations   **8.** specialist / expert   **9.** backing
/ support   **10.** notion / idea   **11.** parts / components   **12.** achievement / accomplishment   **13.** ultimatum / final demand
14. disparity / difference   **15.** proceeds / earnings   **16.** argument / dispute   **17.** amenities / facilities   **18.** display / exhibit
19. implication / suggestion   **20.** reflection / sign

Note that many of the words in this exercise might have another meaning if used in a different context. Use a dictionary to check which ones.

When you keep a written record of words that you learn, you might find it useful to put them into related groups. This would include putting words with the same or a similar meaning together. Remember that you should also record words in context (in other words, you should show how they work in a sentence with other words)

Similar meanings: Verbs 1 (pages 54 – 56)

Across:
2. direct   **4.** assume   **5.** attain   **6.** detect   **11.** reveal   **12.** assert   **13.** resist   **14.** refine   **15.** evolve   **16.** convey
19. settle   **21.** relate   **23.** submit   **25.** change   **27.** baffle   **29.** answer   **32.** verify   **33.** enrich   **35.** remove
36. exceed   **37.** derive

Down:
1. accuse   **3.** handle   **7.** create   **8.** elicit   **9.** forbid   **10.** hasten   **12.** affect   **14.** refuse   **17.** gather   **18.** oblige
(usually used in the passive form: "*Under the college rules, students are obliged to refrain…*")   **20.** endure   **22.** obtain
24. misuse   **26.** assist   **28.** launch   **30.** mirror   **31.** demand   **34.** permit

Note that some of the words above could have a different meaning in another context. For example, in number 8 down, *elicit* has a similar meaning to obtain. In another context, it could mean "*to make someone react in a particular way*" (for example, "*His comments elicited a positive response from everyone in the room*"). This is one reason why you should always record the new words that you meet in context, and with an example that shows how they are used. That way, when you use these words yourself, you use them correctly. A good dictionary with sample sentences is extremely useful in this respect.

Similar meanings: Verbs 2 (pages 57 – 59)

Exercise 1
1. crush   **2.** heighten   **3.** attract   **4.** replacing   **5.** exemplifies   **6.** supported   **7.** recover   **8.** explain   **9.** exhaust
10. achieve   **11.** prevented   **12.** portray   **13.** measure   **14.** encourage   **15.** highlight   **16.** hastened

Exercise 2
1. proved   **2.** solve   **3.** increase   **4.** include   **5.** dictated   **6.** forfeit   **7.** created   **8.** control   **9.** encouraging
10. produce   **11.** suspect   **12.** protect   **13.** constrained   **14.** accepted   **15.** check   **16.** exhibit

Exercise 3
1. realized   **2.** prospered   **3.** surpassed   **4.** understood   **5.** improved   **6.** address   **7.** relating   **8.** originated
9. manage   **10.** examined   **11.** remove   **12.** supposed   **13.** produce   **14.** achieve   **15.** settled   **16.** build

Answer key

Note that while all of these words have a similar meaning to the underlined words in the sentences, not all of them could be used to *replace* those words without partly changing the meaning of the sentence.

Spelling (page 60)

Exercise 1
Apart from **condemning** tobacco companies and **raising** the price of cigarettes, the **government's** anti-smoking **campaign** has failed to have any long-term **effects**, and the only people **benefiting** from it are the Treasury **Department**. Meanwhile, the some doctors have said that they may refuse to treat **persistent** smokers. Of course, this hasn't prevented the big **tobacco companies** spending vast amounts of money on **advertising**.

Exercise 2
It is **arguable** whether good **pronunciation** is more important than good **grammar** and **vocabulary**. **Conscientious** students balance their **acquisition** of these skills, **hoping** to **achieve** both fluency and **accuracy**. Teachers should encourage **their** students to practice* all the **relevant** language skills.

* *Practice* is a noun <u>and</u> a verb in American English. In British English, practi<u>c</u>e is the noun and practi<u>s</u>e is the verb.

Exercise 3
It is **becoming** increasingly **difficult** for many to find decent **accommodations** in Los Angeles at a price they can afford. To put it **simply**, most people just don't have the **necessary** funds. **Organizations** such as *Home Front* can offer **advice**, but it is widely agreed that the situation is no longer **manageable**. The fact that the LA city council is building cheap, **temporary** housing for lower-paid **professionals** is the only official **acknowledgment** of this problem.

Exercise 4
1. reversible   **2.** professional   **3.** criticize   **4.** necessary   **5.** beginning   **6.** perceive   **7.** indispensable   **8.** referring
9. liaison   **10.** tendency   **11.** definitely   **12.** embarrass   **13.** ✓   **14.** ✓   **15.** responsible   **16.** separate   **17.** questionnaire
18. minuscule   **19.** integrate   **20.** ✓   **21.** weird   **22.** irresistible   **23.** achievement   **24.** millennium   **25.** occurrence
26. independent   **27.** supersede   **28.** harassment

Starting and stopping (pages 61 – 62)

The words in the box are:
abolish   arise   back out   cancel   cease   closure   delete   deter   discontinue   dismiss   dissuade   embark   eradicate   establish   expel   fire   freeze   inception   initiate   kick off   launch   outbreak   phase in   phase out   quash   quit   resign   retire   set off   shut down   suppress   suspend   take off   take up   terminate   turn down

1. canceled   **2.** deleted   **3.** backed out *or* pulled out   **4.** outbreak   **5.** set up *or* established / shut down   **6.** embarking *or* setting off   **7.** suppress *or* quash   **8.** eradicated   **9.** deter *or* prevent   **10.** dissuade / initiated   **11.** launched / took off   **12.** suspended   **13.** took up   **14.** phased in / phased out   **15.** inception / closure   **16.** ceased   **17.** retiring   **18.** quit (= informal) *or* resign / fired (= informal) *or* dismissed   **19.** turn…down   **20.** freeze   **21.** discontinued   **22.** abolish   **23.** kick off (= informal)   **24.** arisen   **25.** expelled

Task commands (pages 63 – 64)

Across:
2. identify   **4.** account (in this context, this is part of a phrasal verb: *to account for*)   **6.** argue   **8.** trace   **9.** estimate
12. compare   **13.** define   **15.** illustrate   **16.** assess   **17.** predict   **18.** examine

Down:
1. outline   **3.** elaborate (in this context, this is part of a phrasal verb: *to elaborate on*)   **5.** summarize   **7.** demonstrate
10. evaluate   **11.** analyze   **13.** discuss   **14.** justify

Note that many of the first sentences in each sentence pair in this exercise sound rather long and "awkward". The use of the task command words in the exercise help to shorten and simplify the original sentences.

Time (pages 65 – 66)

Exercise 1
Part 1.
1. prior to (this expression is usually followed by a noun or by an *-ing* verb. For example: *Prior to visiting to country, he had to study the language*)   **2.** By the time   **3.** Formerly / Previously   **4.** precede   **5.** Previously   **6.** Previously / Earlier
Part 2.
1. While / As / Just as (*While* is usually used to talk about long actions. *When* is usually used to talk about short actions: *While we were working*, the phone rang / We were working *when the phone rang*)   **2.** During / Throughout (*During* must always be followed by a noun. *Throughout* can be used on its own. *During the concert*, I fell asleep. / I slept *throughout*)
3. In the meantime / Meanwhile   **4.** At that very moment
Part 3.
1. Following (this word is always followed by a noun. We can also say *After*. *Following / After the movie*, we went home)
2. As soon as / Once / The minute that (these words and expressions are always followed by an action: *As soon as the lecture ended, we left the building*)   **3.** Afterward

Exercise 2
The past:
in medieval times   back in the 1990s   in those days   a few decades ago   at the turn of the century
in my childhood / youth   last century   from 1996 to 1998
The past leading to the present:
ever since   over the past six weeks   lately   for the past few months
The present:
as things stand   nowadays   at this moment in time   at this point in history   these days
The future:
for the next few weeks   one day   from now on   over the coming weeks and months   in another five years' time
by the end of this year   for the foreseeable future   sooner or later

Exercise 3
1. = (q): to make some of your time available for a particular purpose.   **2.** = (o): to like someone or something a lot.
3. = (a): someone or something that is in a time warp seems old-fashioned because they have not changed when other people and things have changed.   **4.** = (s) or (f): to make some of your time available for a particular purpose. This expression is often used in the negative.   **5.** = (n): earlier than necessary.   **6.** = (t): a spoken expression used for saying that someone should do something now, instead of waiting to do it later.   **7.** = (e): an expression that s usually spoken, which means that you are annoyed because something has happened later than it should.   **8.** = (b): usually.   **9.** = (r): used for telling someone to hurry.   **10.** = (d): used for talking about what will happen at some future time.   **11.** = (i): a spoken expression used for saying that you will know in the future whether something is true or right.   **12.** = (p): to make time seem to pass more quickly by doing something instead of just waiting.   **13.** = (j): to change and become modern.
14. = (c): used for saying that something is strange or surprising.   **15.** = (l): the second time that something happens. Also *the first time around, the third time around*, etc.   **16.** = (m): much more modern or advanced than other people or things.
17. = (h): sometimes, but not often.   **18.** = (g): for the present.   **19.** = (k): for a long period of time.   **20.** = (f): used for talking about things that happen fairly often.

Word association 1: Adjectives (pages 67 – 68)

1. careful   **2.** central   **3.** critical   **4.** damaging   **5.** essential   **6.** false   **7.** important   **8.** impossible   **9.** interested
10. lengthy   **11.** major   **12.** material   **13.** modest   **14.** noticeable   **15.** objective   **16.** particular   **17.** popular
18. positive   **19.** rapid   **20.** rational   **21.** realistic   **22.** severe

Word association 2: Nouns (Pages 69 – 71)

Across:
1. background   **5.** effect   **7.** accent   **8.** guess   **11.** advice   **12.** consideration   **14.** suggestion   **15.** instruction
17. solution   **19.** permission   **20.** difficulty   **21.** qualification   **22.** opportunity   **25.** estimate   **29.** appeal   **32.** evidence
33. medicine   **34.** reason

Down:
2. accident   **3.** responsibility   **4.** agreement   **6.** features   **9.** behavior   **10.** career   **12.** contribution   **13.** description
16. criticism   **18.** investigation   **23.** respect   **24.** method   **26.** sequence   **27.** judgment   **28.** project   **30.** progress
31. lesson

Answer key

Word association 3: Verbs (pages 72 – 74)

Exercise 1
1. influence   **2.** obtain   **3.** discuss   **4.** settle   **5.** encourage   **6.** highlight   **7.** devise   **8.** uncover   **9.** deserve
The word in the shaded vertical strip is *undermine*.

Exercise 2
1. inspire   **2.** object   **3.** argue   **4.** oppose   **5.** fight   **6.** highlight   **7.** change   **8.** undertake   **9.** differ
The word in the shaded vertical strip is *negotiate*.

Exercise 3
1. approve   **2.** listen   **3.** dismiss   **4.** abandon   **5.** fall   **6.** combat   **7.** underline   **8.** conclude   **9.** overcome
The word in the shaded vertical strip is *reinforce*.

Word forms 1: Nouns from verbs (pages 75 – 76)

Exercise 1

Remove 2 letters, then add 4 letters:	provide = provision persuade = persuasion recognize = recognition abolish = abolition decide = decision
Remove 1 letter, then add 7 letters:	qualify = qualification apply = application identify = identification notify = notification imply = implication
Remove 1 letter, then add 5 letters:	consume = consumption admire = admiration permit = permission determine = determination compete = competition
Remove 1 letter, then add 4 letters:	argue = argument assure = assurance intervene = intervention expand = expansion produce = production
Remove 1 letter, then add 3 letters:	negotiate = negotiation expose = exposure supervise = supervision (*supervisor*, a person who supervises, could also go in the section below) behave = behavior promote = promotion
Remove 1 letter, then add 2 letters:	refuse = refusal survive = survival (or survivor, somebody who survives) arrive = arrival rehearse = rehearsal respond = response
Add 3 letters:	fail = failure coincide = coincidence warn = warning suggest = suggestion prohibit = prohibition
Add 4 letters:	disturb = disturbance attend = attendance require = requirement manage = management (a *manager* is somebody who manages, e.g., a company or department) prefer = preference
Add 5 letters:	sign = signature expect = expectation recommend = recommendation consult = consultation relax = relaxation

Exercise 2

1. choice (from *choose*)   **2.** solution (from *solve*)   **3.** emphasis (from *emphasize*)   **4.** subscription (from *subscribe*)
5. scrutiny (from *scrutinize*)   **6.** proof (from *prove*)   **7.** criticism (from *criticize*)   **8.** acquisition (from *acquire*)   **9.** loss (from *lose*)   **10.** maintenance (from *maintain*)

The verb / noun in the shaded strip is *compromise*.

Word forms 2: Nouns from adjectives (pages 77 – 78)

Exercise 1
1. value   **2.** taste   **3.** thirst   **4.** honesty   **5.** confidence   **6.** expense   **7.** restrictions   **8.** similarities   **9.** certainty
10. absenteeism (or *absence*)   **11.** convenience   **12.** necessity   **13.** relaxation   **14.** flexibility   **15.** safety
16. responsibility   **17.** accuracy   **18.** profession   **19.** complications   **20.** difference   **21.** charisma   **22.** addiction

23. Constitution (note that this particular example begins with a capital letter)   **24.** investigation   **25.** justification
26. reality

Exercise 2
Remove 4 letters: comfortable = comfort   fashionable = fashion   systematic = system
Remove 3 letters, then add 3 letters: high = height   long = length   strong = strength
Remove 3 letters, then add 1 letter: optimistic = optimism   pessimistic = pessimism   realistic = realism (*reality* is also a noun form)
Remove 2 letters, then add 5 letters: able = ability   available = availability   compatible = compatibility
Remove 2 letters, then add 3 letters: confused = confusion   deep = depth   hot = heat
Remove 2 letters, then add 2 letters: aggressive = aggression   creative = creation   appreciative = appreciation
Remove 2 letters: functional = function   logical = logic   optional = option
Remove 1 letter, then add 3 letters: considerate = consideration   mature = maturity   secure = security
Remove 1 letter, then add 2 letters: convenient = convenience   sufficient = sufficiency   true = truth
Add 2 letters: bored = boredom   loyal = loyalty   warm = warmth
Add 3 letters: familiar = familiarity   popular = popularity   punctual = punctuality
Add 4 letters: aware = awareness   serious = seriousness   weak = weakness

Word forms 3: Adjectives from verbs (page 79)

1. promotional / inspiring   **2.** innovative / impressive   **3.** wasteful / obligatory   **4.** repetitive / boring   **5.** excited / doubtful
6. decisive / active   **7.** inventive / changeable   **8.** continual (= stopping and starting) / continuous (without stopping)
9. approachable / frightening   **10.** convincing / critical   **11.** inclusive / competitive   **12.** helpful / supportive / dependable
13. rectifiable / preferable   **14.** negotiable / refundable   **15.** restricted / valid   **16.** voluntary / constructive   **17.** avoidable
/ careless (not *careful*)   **18.** creative / imaginative / admirable   **19.** specific / occupational   **20.** attractive / excellent
21. contradictory / enthusiastic   **22.** active / preferable

Working words (pages 80 – 81)

Exercise 1
1. to / no / of   **2.** ago / used *or* had / These   **3.** even   **4.** Between / almost *or* about *or* over   **5.** most *or* some / near
6. be / on   **7.** Unless / on *or* for   **8.** at / many / would   **9.** spite / managed   **10.** This / on   **11.** who / just *or* recently
12. with / made   **13.** by / had   **14.** the / where   **15.** By / had / that / off   **16.** been / for / no / it

Exercise 2
1. give / until / two / these   **2.** least / more / because *or* as *or* since / had   **3.** with / from / This / on   **4.** which / the / one
/ the   **5.** until / would, could *or* might / they / to / or   **6.** of / to / a / on   **7.** the *or* a / in / where   **8.** Between / from / they
/ to   **9.** or / most / near / that *or* which   **10.** only / if, provided *or* providing / least / unless   **11.** on / be / little *or* lot / now
12. at *or* in / for / in   **13.** what / from / was / at *or* on   **14.** that / as / of / anyone *or* everyone   **15.** with / did / made

Children and the family (pages 82 – 83)

Exercise 1
1. Adolescence / adolescent   **2.** minor   **3.** siblings   **4.** separated / divorced   **5.** foster family / foster child / foster
6. juvenile   **7.** well-adjusted / running wild *or* rebellious   **8.** formative years   **9.** adopt   **10.** teenager   **11.** infant / infancy
12. Raise / bring up   **13.** extended family / nuclear family   **14.** strict / authoritarian / lenient   **15.** dependent (note that
in British English, the noun is *dependant*)

Exercise 3
1. formative years   **2.** divorced   **3.** brought up   **4.** foster family   **5.** authoritarian / strict   **6.** upbringing   **7.** running
wild   **8.** adolescence   **9.** juvenile delinquency   **10.** responsible   **11.** siblings   **12.** well-adjusted   **13.** lenient   **14.** over-
protective   **15.** nuclear family   **16.** single-parent family   **17.** dependents   **18.** extended

Education (pages 84 – 85)

Exercise 1
1. correspondence course / night class / day release   **2.** SAT   **3.** lesson / class (in either order)   **4.** lecture / subject *or* topic
/ lecturer / seminar / tutorial / tutor   **5.** Literacy / Numeracy   **6.** prospectus / enroll (the British-English spelling is *enrol*)
7. faculty   **8.** Physical education   **9.** public school / private school / fees*   **10.** kindergarten / grade / elementary school

/ grade school   **11.** syllabus   **12.** junior high school / middle school (in either order) / high school   **13.** semester / quarter
14. graduate / graduate school / higher degree

*Note that in the U.K., a public school is a school for children whose parents pay for their education. In the U.S.A., a public school is a free local school controlled and paid for by the government.

Exercise 3
1. skills   **2 / 3.** literacy / numeracy (in either order)   **4.** kindergarten / elementary school   **5.** elementary   **6.** secondary
7. discipline   **8.** pass   **9.** qualifications   **10.** acquire   **11.** physical education   **12.** graduate   **13.** higher   **14.** degree
15. subject   **16.** graduate school   **17.** doctorate   **18.** night class   **19.** day release   **20.** correspondence course
21. mature   **22.** opportunity

Food and diet (pages 86 – 87)

Exercise 1
1. Fiber (spelt *fibre* in British English) / fat / saturated / monosaturated   **2.** Calories / Protein / Calcium / Carbohydrates
3. diet / fat farm / exercise   **4.** Organic / Free range / Genetically modified (*GM*)   **5.** eating disorder / bulimia / anorexia
(these last two in either order)   **6.** vegetarian / vegan   **7.** Fast food / junk food / nutritious   **8.** overweight / obese / obesity
/ diabetes / heart disease   **9.** salmonella / listeria (in either order) / food poisoning   **10.** food groups   **11.** balanced diet
12. food intolerance / allergy / allergic

Exercise 2
1. fast food   **2 / 3.** minerals / vitamins (in either order)   **4 / 5.** fat / carbohydrates (in either order)   **6.** malnutrition
7. scarcity   **8.** harvest   **9.** balanced diet   **10.** fiber   **11.** fat / cholesterol   **12.** calories   **13.** genetically modified
14. organic   **15 / 16.** salmonella / listeria (in either order)   **17.** food poisoning

The media (pages 88 – 89)

Exercise 1
1. slander (this can also be a verb: *to slander someone*) / slanderous / libel (this can also be a verb: *to libel someone*) /
libelous   **2.** read between the lines   **3.** invasion of privacy   **4.** broadsheet / tabloid / gutter press / tabloid TV (note that
several newspapers that were previously printed on large sheets of paper are now printed on smaller sheets of paper, with
the result that broadsheet is not used so much any more. It is becoming increasingly common to refer to the old
broadsheets as *quality papers*, and tabloids as *popular papers*)   **5.** dumbing down   **6.** journalist / reporter (also known as
a *correspondent*)   **7.** censorship (the verb is *to censor*)   **8.** media tycoon (also called a *media baron*)   **9.** reality TV
10. documentary / current affairs   **11.** check book journalism   **12.** airtime / coverage / readership

Exercise 3
1. informed   **2.** broadsheets   **3.** coverage   **4.** current affairs   **5.** journalists *or* reporters   **6.** reporters *or* journalists
7. tabloids   **8.** broadcasts *or* programs   **9.** documentaries   **10.** Internet   **11.** websites   **12.** download   **13.** information
or entertainment   **14.** entertainment *or* information   **15.** gutter press   **16.** invasion of privacy   **17.** paparazzi   **18.** libel
19. check book journalism   **20.** unscrupulous   **21.** dumbing down   **22.** reality TV   **23.** online   **24.** censorship /
restrictions   **25.** freedom of the press

Money and finance (pages 90 – 91)

Exercise 1
1. expenditure   **2.** borrow   **3.** refund   **4.** bankrupt   **5.** balance   **6.** in the black   **7.** receipt   **8.** loss   **9.** exorbitant
10. invest   **11.** salary   **12.** priceless   **13.** withdraw   **14.** overcharged   **15.** frugal *or* economical   **16.** check   **17.** debit
18. savings and loan association   **19.** mortgage   **20.** overdraft

Exercise 3
1. borrow   **2.** loan   **3.** income   **4.** expenditure   **5.** overdraft   **6.** cost of living   **7.** inflation   **8.** economize
9. savings and loan association   **10.** interest   **11.** on credit   **12.** exorbitant   **13.** save   **14.** reductions   **15.** bargain
16. discount   **17.** invest   **18.** stocks   **19.** shares   **20.** priceless

Nature and the environment (pages 93 – 94)

Exercise 1
1. green belt   **2.** biodegradable packaging   **3.** greenhouse gases   **4.** rain forest   **5.** erosion   **6.** recycle   **7.** organic
8. genetically modified (often shortened to *GM*)   **9.** unleaded gas   **10.** Acid rain   **11.** ecosystem   **12.** emissions / fossil
fuels   **13.** contaminated (or *polluted*)   **14.** environmentalists   **15.** Global warming

Exercise 3
1. fossil fuels   **2.** acid rain   **3.** greenhouse gases / CFC gases   **4.** global warming   **5.** rainforest   **6.** contaminated
7. emissions / gases / fumes   **8.** poaching   **9.** endangered species   **10.** ecosystem   **11.** recycle   **12.** biodegradable
packaging   **13.** genetically modified   **14.** organic   **15.** unleaded gas   **16.** environmentalists   **17.** conservation programs
18. battery farming   **19.** green belts

On the road (pages 95 – 96)

Exercise 1
1. Wrong. *Rush hour* is the time of day when there are a lot of vehicles on the road because most people are traveling to
or from work.   **2.** Wrong. <u>Part</u> of its operating costs are paid for by the government or a local authority.   **3.** Wrong. In
the USA, a *traffic school* is a school where drivers are sent to correct their bad driving (usually offered as an alternative to
another form of punishment such as a *fine* or *prison sentence* when the driver has done something dangerous or caused
an accident).   **4.** Correct.   **5.** Correct.   **6.** Wrong. *Traffic calming* refers to methods used to slow down traffic in towns
and cities (for example, by building raised areas across roads). It is a British-English expression that is becoming more widely
used in the USA.   **7.** Wrong. The *interstate* is a wide road with several lanes of traffic going in each direction, built for fast
travel over long distances as part of a national road system.   **8.** Correct.   **9.** Correct.   **10.** Wrong. *Back out* is another
expression for to *reverse* (to move a car backward).   **11.** Correct.   **12.** Wrong. A *traffic-free zone* is an area where you
cannot drive a vehicle (including, in some cases and at some times, bicycles).   **13.** Wrong. *Fatalities* are people who are
killed in accidents on the road.   **14.** Correct   **15.** Correct   **16.** Wrong. A *sidewalk* is an area to the side of a road where
people can walk.

Exercise 3
1 / 2. injuries / fatalities (in either order)   **3.** speeding   **4.** speed limit   **5.** drunk driving   **6.** pedestrians   **7.** crosswalks
8. traffic light   **9 / 10.** congestion / pollution (in either order)   **11.** black spot   **12.** transport strategy   **13.** Traffic-
calming   **14.** Park and ride   **15.** traffic-free zone / pedestrian mall   **16.** cycle lanes   **17.** subsidized   **18.** fines
19. dominate   **20.** traffic school

Science and technology (pages 97 – 98)

Exercise 1
1. Genetic engineering   **2.** safeguard (this can also be a verb: to *safeguard*)   **3.** Biology (the adjective is *biological*. A
scientist who studies living things is a *biologist*)   **4.** technophobe (the fear or distrust of technology is called *technophobia*.
A *technophile* is someone who is very enthusiastic about technology)   **5.** breakthrough   **6.** Information technology
7. modified   **8.** geneticist   **9.** Cybernetics   **10.** technocrat   **11.** Research (this can also be a verb: to *research*)
12. Cryogenics   **13.** experiment (this can also be a verb: to *experiment*. The adjective is *experimental*)   **14.** Life expectancy
15. Innovation (the verb is to *innovate*. The adjective is *innovative*)

Exercise 3
1. discovered   **2.** life expectancy   **3.** innovations / inventions   **4.** breakthrough   **5.** invented   **6.** Internet   **7.** e-mail
8. research   **9.** technophiles   **10.** technophobes   **11.** cybernetics   **12.** nuclear engineering   **13.** safeguards
14. genetic engineering   **15.** analyzed   **16.** experiment   **17.** control

Town and country (pages 99 – 100)

Exercise 1 (the letters in **bold** show you the letters that need to go in the grid)
1. prospe**c**ts   **2.** metr**o**polis   **3.** infra**s**tructure   **4.** co**m**muter   **5.** **o**utskirts   **6.** de**p**opulation   **7.** c**o**ngestion   **8.** me**l**ting
pot   **9.** m**i**gration   **10.** s**t**ressful   **11.** urb**a**n (the opposite is *rural*)   **12.** ame**n**ities

The word that fits in the grid is *cosmopolitan*.

Answer key

Exercise 3

1. metropolis   **2.** cosmopolitan   **3.** urban   **4.** amenities / facilities   **5.** cultural events   **6.** infrastructure   **7.** commuters
8. Central Business District   **9.** rush hour / peak periods   **10.** congestion / traffic jams   **11.** pollution   **12.** cost of living
13. building sites   **14.** population explosion   **15.** drug abuse / street crime   **16.** inner city   **17.** rural   **18.** prospects
19. productive land / cultivation / arable land   **20.** urban sprawl   **21.** environment

Travel (pages 101 – 102)

Exercise 1

1. *Persona non grata* is a Latin expression that is used in English. It is most commonly used to refer to someone who is not allowed in a country because they do not have formal permission to be there (for example, their visa for that country has expired, or their passport is no longer valid)   **2.** culture shock   **3.** A *travel agent* is someone whose job is to help people plan holidays and make travel arrangements (they usually work for a *travel agency*). A *tour operator* is a company that organizes holiday tours and then sells them, usually through a travel agency.   **4.** excursion   **5.** coach class (called *economy* or *tourist class* in British English) / first class / business class (sometimes also called by other names, including *Club Class*)
6. You would probably not be happy. If you are *deported*, you are sent out of the country you are in (maybe because you have done something wrong)   **7.** mass tourism   **8.** A *package tourist* goes on a *package tour*, where they pay for all flights, transfers, accommodation, etc., together and in advance, usually through a travel agency. An *independent traveler* books different aspects of their trip separately (for example, they might book their flight on the Internet, then get a taxi from the airport to their hotel, pay for their hotel when they arrive at their destination, etc.) and does not usually rely on an agency   **9.** No. A *refugee* is someone who leaves their country because they have to (usually because of a war or other threatening event). An *expatriate* is someone who chooses to live and work in another country   **10.** UNHCR = *United Nations High Commission for Refugees*, the department of the United Nations that deals with the problem of refugees (see number 9) and other displaced people (= people who have been forcibly moved from their home, town, country, etc.: see number 16)   **11.** Ecotourism (also called *green tourism* or sometimes *responsible tourism*)   **12.** Someone who has been *repatriated* has been sent back from one country to the country that is legally their own (possibly because they have been *deported* – see number 6).   **13.** A *cruise* is a journey on a ship for pleasure, especially one that involves visiting a series of places. A *safari* is a journey taken in order to watch or take pictures of wild animals   **14.** A person who is not from the U.S.A., but wants to live and work there: a *green card* is an official document that allows them to do this.   **15.** They are doing something that is illegal: *trafficking* involves buying and selling things such as drugs and weapons illegally, usually between countries.   **16.** internally displaced

Exercise 3

1. travel agent   **2.** package tour   **3.** independent travelers   **4.** visas   **5.** check in   **6.** coach class   **7.** disembark
8. mass tourism   **9.** all-inclusive   **10.** ecotourism   **11.** refugees   **12.** internally displaced   **13.** economic migrants
14. expatriates   **15.** culture shock   **16.** immigration   **17.** persona non grata   **18.** deported   **19.** checking in
20. excursion

Work (pages 103 – 104)

Exercise 1

1. applicant   **2.** A *wage* and a *salary* are both money you receive for doing a job, but the first is usually paid daily or weekly and the second is usually paid monthly   **3.** Repetitive strain injury (usually abbreviated to *RSI*)   **4.** fired   **5.** increment
6. A *blue-collar worker* does work that involves physical strength or skill with their hands (for example, in a factory or a mine) and a *white-collar worker* works in an office   **7.** False. It makes some of its workers *redundant* (=it gets rid of some of its workers) because it no longer needs them   **8.** perks   **9.** *Sick building syndrome* is a medical condition that affects people who work in buildings where the air is not healthy   **10.** a steady job   **11.** False. When you *retire*, you stop working because you have reached a particular age. When you *resign*, you leave a job because (for example) you want a different job or because you are not happy with the company you are working for   **12.** service industries   **13.** No. Your work conditions are bad (for example, you might not have much job security, your place of work might be unhealthy or dangerous, etc.)   **14.** freelance (This can also be a verb: *to freelance*. The person who does this is called a *freelancer*)

Exercise 3

1. employees   **2.** unskilled   **3.** semi-skilled   **4.** blue-collar   **5.** manufacturing industries   **6.** white-collar   **7.** service industries   **8.** job security   **9.** steady job   **10.** hiring   **11.** firing   **12.** stress   **13.** demanding   **14.** unsociable hours
15. repetitive strain injury   **16.** salary   **17.** promotion   **18.** perks   **19.** incentive   **20.** increment / raise   **21.** sickness benefit   **22.** pension   **23.** self-employed